THE SEEGE OF TROYE

&

THE RAWLINSON PROSE SIEGE OF TROY

Works by D. M. Smith

Munley Priory: A Gothic Story
The Cypria: Reconstructing the Lost Prequel to Homer's Iliad
The Telegony: Rediscovering the Lost Epilogue to Homer's Odyssey

The Troy Myth in Medieval Britain

I. John Lydgate's Troy Book: A Middle English Iliad
II. The Seege of Troye & The Rawlinson Prose Siege of Troy
III. The Laud Troy Book: The Forgotten Troy Romance
IV. The Recueil of the Histories of Troy: The First English Book
V. The Destruction of Troy by John Clerk of Whalley: The Gest Hystoriale

Follow **@d.m.smith.authorpage** on Facebook to interact with the author and receive information on upcoming titles.

TWO SHORTER ACCOUNTS OF THE TROJAN WAR:

THE SEEGE OF TROYE

&

THE RAWLINSON PROSE SIEGE OF TROY

A MODERN TRANSLATION BY D. M. SMITH

ISBN: 9781091512306

To Charles H. A. Wager,
Mary E. Barnicle & Nathaniel E. Griffin,
upon whose shoulders I stand

CONTENTS

FOREWORD

Foreword to "The Troy Myth in Medieval Britain"

It is difficult to conceive of a time when the twin pillars of Homer's *Iliad* and *Odyssey* did not loom over the Western literary canon. Perhaps surprisingly, the Homeric poems did not arrive in Western Europe until relatively late, with English, French and German translations not appearing until the end of the sixteenth century. Prior to this the story of the Trojan War was transmitted through a variety of medieval poems and prose works, drawn from the Late Latin "histories" of Dictys Cretensis and Dares Phrygius. His works unremembered, Homer was a name only—dismissed as a teller of tall tales which placed gods on the battlefield, and displayed a heavy bias towards his native Greece.

In his absence, the legend was free to grow and evolve for several centuries into a thoroughly medieval story—replete with chivalrous knights and courtly romance—until it scarcely resembled the Bronze Age myths of old. These texts are largely overlooked today, removed as they are from the traditional narrative. They represent a cul-de-sac in the evolution of the Trojan War mythos, rendered defunct with the re-emergence of Homer in the early modern period.

Few would argue that any of these medieval works rank alongside their classical forebears in terms of their quality, but that is not to say they should be dismissed out of hand. An important aspect of the medieval Troy story is that it considers the conflict as a whole, in contrast with today's narrow focus on the two Homeric poems, and the various episodes described in the works of Virgil, Ovid, and others. The

Iliad, for example, recounts mere weeks of a war that lasted a decade. This gave medieval audiences a broader understanding of the tradition, with non-Homeric characters such as Troilus, Palamedes, Neoptolemus, Memnon and Penthesilea much more prominent. Now, with so much of the classical material having been lost, the medieval epics of Benoît de Sainte-Maure and John Lydgate allow a reader to explore the wider story in a level of detail not possible with the surviving Graeco-Roman classics.

The actual Trojan War—if it does indeed have any historical basis—is generally placed at around 1200 BC, corresponding with evidence of a deliberate destruction at Hissarlik (the probable site of ancient Ilium). The literary history begins some four centuries after, emerging from an earlier, oral tradition. Rather than describing a specific conflict, it may be that the legendary destruction of Troy and the scattering of the returning Greeks represents the disintegration of the Mycenaean and Hittite kingdoms in Greece and Anatolia which occurred at the beginning of the twelfth century BC, otherwise known as the "Bronze Age collapse".

The wider story of the Trojan War was told in a "cycle" of eight epic poems, beginning with the *Cypria*, which told of the wedding of Peleus and Thetis and the abduction of Helen, and ending with the *Telegony*, sequel to the *Odyssey*, which described the last years of Ulysses and his death at the hands of his estranged son Telegonus. The six "Cyclic" epics (so-named as to distinguish them from the "Homeric") are thought to be a century or so younger than the *Iliad* and *Odyssey*, although they derive from the same oral tradition. Criticised by Hellenistic scholars as formulaic and inferior to the Homeric epics, the Cyclic poems were held in less regard, and by the end of the classical era survived only in fragments quoted by other authors.

Today, the stories of these lost epics are contained within the works of later writers. In the fourth century, Quintus of Smyrna incorporated the *Aethiopis*, *Little Iliad* and *Iliou Persis* ("Fall of Troy") into his *Posthomerica*, and a part of the lost *Nostoi* ("Returns") is told in the *Oresteia*—a trilogy of plays written by Aeschylus in the fifth century BC. A Latin retelling of the *Iliou Persis* can also be found in Book II of Virgil's *Aeneid.*

By Late Antiquity the epic poem was no longer the preferred mode of storytelling, with an early form of the novel beginning to appear in the first and second centuries. Two prose "histories" of the war survive from this period, purporting to be the first-hand accounts of actual participants. These deviate from the traditional, Homeric narrative in ways that seem deliberate, rather than (as some have suggested) the result of a reliance on obscure, Late Classical sources. Anything expressly magical, divine, or supernatural has been excised, in order to present them as "genuine" histories, in contrast with the mythological retellings of the poets.

Dictys Cretensis Ephemeris Belli Trojani ("Dictys the Cretan's Chronicle of the Trojan War") is written as the recollections of one Dictys of Crete, veteran of the Trojan War and subject of King Idomeneus. Dictys' narrative spans the entire Epic Cycle from the *Cypria* to the *Telegony*, beginning with the abduction of Helen and ending with the death of Ulysses. It was published in Latin in the fourth century AD by a Lucius Septimius, prefaced with a somewhat fanciful epistle detailing its discovery in Dictys' earthquake-damaged tomb at Cnossos during the reign of the Emperor Nero (54–68 AD). The text, in Phoenician letters, was reportedly inscribed on a number of wooden tablets preserved in a tin box; this was subsequently translated into Greek and presented as a gift to Nero. Three centuries later it was rendered in Latin by Septimius, who describes condensing nine books into six by combining and abridging the final four—those devoted to the Returns of the Greeks and the adventures of Ulysses.

For many years it was assumed that the Latin version was in fact the original, with Septimius presenting it as the translation of an ancient text to lend an air of authenticity to his narrative. However, in the winter of 1899–1900 fragments of a Greek original were discovered among the ruins of the Egyptian city of Tebtunis, written on the back of a revenue return dated 206 AD.* This proved once and for all that Septimius was indeed the translator of an earlier Greek work—even if the story of its discovery in a tomb is almost certainly spurious! Sadly, none of the Greek fragments come from the later books that Septimius claimed to have abridged, so we are unable to say conclusively that the original text was longer. This said, Byzantine writings on the Returns of the Greeks known to derive from Dictys do contain details not present in the extant version.

Daretis Phrygii de Excidio Trojae Historia ("Dares of Phrygia's History of the Destruction of Troy") claims to be the writings of Dares the Phrygian, a Trojan priest who is actually mentioned in Book V of Homer's *Iliad* when his son Phegeus is slain by Diomedes. The Roman author Aelian (c. 175–c. 235 AD) wrote of an "Iliad of Dares" in his *Varia Historia* that predated Homer's epic, but the *Excidio Trojae* is clearly a Late Latin counterfeit, with the original either lost or never having existed.† As with Dictys, the *Excidio Trojae* begins with a translator's note—in this case entirely fictional. It is presented as the work of the Roman biographer Cornelius Nepos (c. 110–c. 25 BC), but the style of Latin would suggest a date of the fifth or sixth century AD.

Dares' *Excidio Trojae Historia* is described by Nathaniel Edward Griffin as "an ill-assorted aggregation of meagre details, written in forty-four chapters of barbarous Latin."‡ It begins with an account of the quest for the Golden Fleece, which results in the Argonauts sacking Laomedon's Troy in revenge for a hostile reception during their voyage to Colchis. Paris' abduction of Helen then becomes an attempt by Priam to exchange her for his sister Hesione, taken as a concubine by the Greek hero Telamon. The actual siege of Troy occupies roughly half of the narrative, which ends with the sacrifice of Polyxena and the

* Nathaniel Edward Griffin, "The Greek Dictys", *The American Journal of Philology* vol. 29, no. 3 (1900): 329-335

† Claudius Aelianus, *Vara Historia*, XL.2

‡ Nathaniel Edward Griffin, *Dares and Dictys: An Introduction to the Medieval Versions of the Story of Troy* (J. H. Furst Company, 1907): p. 4

departure of the Greeks.

Whilst appearing to be obvious forgeries today—and probably recognised as such at the time of their composition—over time the memoirs of Dictys and Dares came to be accepted as genuine, displacing the patently mythological writings of Homer. Medieval scholars held them in the highest authority, and it was not until the eighteenth century that the historicity of the Trojan War began to be called into question.

In 1934 evidence of a third Latin chronicle—now lost—was presented in a Mediaeval Academy of America journal by E. Bagby Atwood. The *Rawlinson Excidium Troiae* ("Destruction of Troy") is a medieval text of the late thirteenth century, discovered among a collection of manuscripts amassed by eighteenth century antiquarian Richard Rawlinson. The text consists of a short chronicle of the Trojan War, an epitome of Virgil's *Aeneid*, and an account of the founding of Rome. The Latin is very simple and repetitive, with a pattern of questions and answers that would indicate a school exercise or textbook. Despite these unremarkable origins, the Troy story is essentially the classical one, with descriptions of the birth and fostering of Paris among the shepherds of Ida, and the youth of Achilles on Skyros that mark it as "the only complete medieval account of the Trojan War completely independent of Dares and Dictys."* In order to assemble such a narrative, the author would have needed to consult Ovid, Statius, the *Ilias Latina* (a first century Latin summary of Homer's *Iliad*), Hyginus, Servius and others. Atwood deemed it "utterly impossible to suppose a medieval writer capable of selecting and arranging this scattered information in a simple, connected narrative agreeing so closely... with the ancient Epic Cycle." He was thus "forced to conclude that the *Excidium Troiae* is a recension of a considerably older Latin chronicle of the Trojan

* E. Bagby Atwood, "The Rawlinson Excidium Troie – A Study of Source Problems in Mediaeval Troy Literature", *Speculum* vol. 9, no. 4 (1934): p. 379

War."*

The *Roman de Troie* ("Romance of Troy") of Benoît de Sainte-Maure (d. 1173) is aptly described by C. H. A. Wager as the "point of departure for an investigation of the Troy Cycle in the Middle Ages."† All medieval versions of the Troy myth (with the exception of Joseph of Exeter's nearly-contemporary *De Bello Troiano*) in some way derive from this 30,000 word poem, written in French in the 1150s and dedicated to Eleanor of Aquitaine. It was Benoît who first reframed a Bronze Age myth as a medieval romance, replacing chariots with mounted knights, and introducing concepts such as chivalry and courtly love into the barbaric world of Homeric Greece and Asia Minor.

Benoît's narrative is essentially an expansion of the *Excidio Trojae Historia* of Dares, with Books V and VI of Dictys' *Ephemeris belli Trojani* tacked onto the end. There are also hints of Ovid, Hyginus, and perhaps the now-lost Latin source of the *Rawlinson Excidium Troiae*. The fusion of Dares and Dictys is not always a comfortable one, and leads to a number of continuity errors; these must have caused great confusion for those readers over the centuries who did not have access to the source material—characters who die in the "Dares" portion of the text are still alive in the "Dictys" part, and then must die all over again. It is interesting to note that had Benoît relied solely on Dictys, the medieval Troy narrative would not have diverged nearly as far from the original Greek Epic Cycle.

The *Roman de Troie* was at one time believed to be the recension of a larger work; scholars of the nineteenth century wrote of an "enlarged *Roman de Troie*", in order to explain certain details in its derivatives that were not present in Benoît's text. This theory was conclusively disproven with the discovery of the *Rawlinson Excidium*

* Atwood, 389

† Charles Henry Adams Wager (ed.), *The Seege of Troye* (Macmillan, 1899): pp. xvii-xviii

Troiae, which supplies all of the material "missing" from Benoît.

In 1287 the Sicilian judge and writer Guido delle Colonne published a prose work in Latin entitled *Historia Destructionis Troiae* ("History of the Destruction of Troy"). It is described—unflatteringly—by editor Nathaniel Edward Griffin as "an essentially pedestrian piece of work, devoid of any claim to high literary excellence, and extremely wordy."* Guido names his sources as "Dytem Grecum et Frigium Daretem" ("Dictys the Greek and Dares the Phrygian"), but the *Historia* is in fact entirely lifted from Benoît's *Roman de Troie*. It was not until 1869 that German scholar Dr. Hermann Dunger and French philologist Aristide Joly revealed Guido's indebtedness to the *Roman de Troie*, and thus "restored Benoît to his proper fame."†

The earliest-known literary work by an Englishman on the Trojan War is Joseph of Exeter's *De Bello Troiano* ("The Trojan War"): a verse rendering of Dares' *Excidio Trojae* dating from about 1183. *De Bello Troiano* was written in Latin, and it would be another century and a half before such a work appeared in the English language. The Middle English Troy canon is represented by five major poetical works and two prose works, all of which ultimately derive from either Benoît's *Roman de Troie* or Guido's *Historia Destructionis Troiae*, occasionally supplemented with material from Ovid's *Metamorphoses* and the lost Latin work now represented by the *Rawlinson Excidium Troiae*.

The *Seege of Troye* (sometimes *Batayle of Troye*) is the shortest of the five Middle English Troy poems at just under 2,000 lines, and also the earliest, dating from the beginning of the fourteenth century. Four manuscript copies survive, three of which are believed to represent the original poem, with the fourth a rewrite by a later poet. The *Seege* draws primarily from Dares Phrygius and (to a lesser degree) Benoît's

* Nathaniel Edward Griffin (ed.), *Guido de Columnis Historia Destructionis Troiae* (Mediaeval Academy of America, 1935): p. xvi

† Wager (1899), p. xviii

Roman de Troie, but also includes details from the *Rawlinson Excidium Troiae* which proved a major headache for scholars prior to its unearthing in 1934. The poem's brevity and simple language suggest that it was originally set to music, to be performed by a minstrel.

The *Gest Hystoriale of the Destruction of Troy* consists of 14,044 lines of alliterative verse, and is believed to date from the late fourteenth century. It was once ascribed to the semi-mythical poet Huchoun, but the author was identified as one John Clerk of Whalley by Professor Thorlac Turville-Petre in the 1980s, who discovered that the first letters of the first words of the prologue and Books I-XXII spell M IOHANNES CLERK DE WHALALE.* The *Gest* survives in a single (incomplete) manuscript copy, and is a close translation of Guido's *Historia Destructionis Troiae*.

Certainly the most famous of the English Troy poems—and perhaps the only one that is still widely read and studied to this day—is Geoffrey Chaucer's *Troilus and Criseyde*. It consists of 8,239 lines, or 1,177 stanzas of "rhyme royal"—a seven line stanza first introduced by Chaucer—and was composed during the 1380s in the years prior to his *Canterbury Tales*. Chaucer names his source as one "Lollius", presenting something of a puzzle for scholars, as the work is clearly a retelling of Giovanni Boccaccio's *Il Filostrato*—itself based on the non-Homeric love triangle of Troilus, Briseis and Diomedes found in Benoît's *Roman de Troie*. John Lydgate was an ardent admirer, deferring to Chaucer's authority in his own *Troy Book*, and the work later provided inspiration for Shakespeare's *Troilus and Cressida* (c. 1602).

Troy Book is a 30,000 line verse translation of Guido's *Historia Destructionis Troiae* in decasyllabic couplets, completed in the year 1420. Its author was John Lydgate: a monk of Bury St. Edmunds, and one of the major English poets of the fifteenth century. Lydgate greatly expanded Guido's rather bare narrative, interweaving material from

* Thorlac Turville-Petre, "The Author of The Destruction of Troy", *Medium Ævum* vol. 57, no. 2 (1988): p. 264

Ovid's *Metamorphoses* and erotic poetry, as well as his own reflections and moralisations. The work was immensely popular in its day, with the first print edition appearing in 1513, but had fallen out of favour—along with the rest of Lydgate's poetry—by the eighteenth century. In 1614 a "modernised" version of *Troy Book* was published; titled *The Life and Death of Hector,* it is tentatively attributed to the playwright Thomas Heywood.

The *Laud Troy Book* is another verse translation of Guido's *Historia* dating from around 1400, and takes its name from a former owner of the sole manuscript copy, the Archbishop William Laud (b. 1573–d. 1645). Its author is unknown, although for many years it was believed to be an alternate version of Lydgate's poem, written in octosyllabic couplets. It covers much the same ground as the Lydgate *Troy Book,* but is roughly a third shorter at 18,664 lines, ending—as does Dares—with the sacrifice of Polyxena and the departure of the Greeks.

The prose *Sege of Troye*—sometimes referred to as the *Rawlinson Prose Siege of Troy* to distinguish it from the poem of the same name—is an anonymous 10,000 word prose summary of Lydgate's *Troy Book*, produced a decade or so after the original. Aside from a few details cribbed from Dares Phrygius it adds nothing to Lydgate's narrative, but does at least have the distinction of being the earliest known prose account of the Trojan War in English, and was for many years supposed to have been translated directly from Guido's *Historia.*

In 1473, William Caxton's *Recuyell of the Historyes of Troye* ("Collection of the Histories of Troy") became the first book to be printed in the English language. Described by H. Oskar Sommer as "the fountain-head of modern literary English",* it was in fact a translation of a French work, the *Recoeil des Histoires de Troyes* written by Raoul Lefévre a decade earlier. The *Recuyell* is much greater in scope than its

* H. Oskar Sommer (ed.), *The Recuyell of the Historyes of Troye* vol. 1 (David Nutt, 1894): p. lxxxiii

title would suggest: Books I and II are devoted to Jupiter's overthrow of Saturn and the deeds of Perseus and Hercules—largely drawn from Giovanni Boccaccio's *Genealogy of the Pagan Gods*—with Guido's account of the Trojan War occupying the third and final book. Despite being "the most inferior... of all English versions",* Caxton's *Recuyell* was widely read and frequently reprinted, receiving fifteen editions between 1473 and 1738.

References to the Trojan War appear in a number of other medieval works, such as John Gower's *Confessio Amantis*, Lydgate's *Fall of Princes*, and the *Chronicle* of Robert Mannyng; none of these quite fit the definition of a "Troy" poem, but one would be remiss not to mention them. Likewise the lost Scottish verse translation of Guido's *Historia* known as the *Scottish Troy Book*, fragments of which are preserved in two independent manuscripts of Lydgate's *Troy Book*. Approximately 3,700 lines survive of this obscure work, which has been dated to around 1400. Nineteenth-century scholars confidently ascribed the work to the poet John Barbour (d. 1395), but there is no evidence supporting this claim.

With the bulk of these texts now either out of print or otherwise difficult to obtain, it is my intention to publish a series of new editions for the twenty-first century, beginning with the Lydgate *Troy Book*, fully annotated and translated into Modern English. My hope is to eventually cover all of the aforementioned works—with the exception perhaps of Chaucer's *Troilus and Criseyde*, of which there seems to be little need for one more edition amongst the multitude!

* Ibid., p. xliv

INTRODUCTION

The Seege of Troye

THE *Seege* or *Batayle of Troye* (titles vary between manuscripts) is thought to have been composed at the beginning of the fourteenth century, making it the earliest surviving work in the English language to describe the Trojan War. Its author is unknown, but editor of the 1927 edition Mary Elizabeth Barnicle makes them a native of the Northwest Midlands via a simple triangulation, with the Midland dialect in the three earliest manuscripts, the Welsh words "crouth" (a stringed instrument) and "cader" (a cradle), and the presence of Northern vowel sounds in many of the rhymes at the three corners.[*] Its age may be gleaned from the descriptions of the weapons and armour, with references to "aketons" (l. 1398) and "hauberks of mail" (l. 1932) and the absence of plate armour placing it firmly in the early 1300s. The foot soldiers also fight with swords and spears, rather than the halberds, pikes, poleaxes and bills which dominated battlefields from the late fourteenth century onwards.[†]

The poem was composed in octosyllabic rhyming couplets with a stress on every second syllable—a metre common to early French romances, which began to appear in English literature in the thirteenth and fourteenth centuries. Frequent repetition of stock phrases and "direct appeals and addresses to the audience"[‡] suggest a minstrel poem,

[*] Mary Elizabeth Barnicle (ed.) *The Seege or Batayle of Troye* (H. Miford, Oxford University Press, 1927): p. xxx

[†] Ibid., p. xxxii

[‡] Ibid., p. xxxiii

originally set to music, and its succinctness would have made it suitable for performance in full. Indeed, it is not difficult to imagine the *Seege of Troye* being performed after a feast in some medieval hall, accompanied by a lyre—or perhaps the Welsh "crouth" mentioned on line 761.

Charles Henry Adams Wager, who edited the Harleian manuscript for the 1899 Early English Text Society edition, believed the *Seege of Troye* to be "little more than a condensed paraphrase" of Benoît's *Roman de Troie*,* although he did concede that the author must have had some knowledge of Dares. A quarter of a century later M. E. Barnicle demonstrated the reverse to be true—the work is chiefly based on the *Excidio Trojae Historia*, citing no less than a hundred lines or couplets that the poet has seemingly lifted (and translated) from Dares Phrygius.† Her findings reflected the opinion of earlier scholars, A. Zietsch (who first published the *Seege* in German philological journal *Archiv* in 1884)‡ and W. Grief, both of whom favoured Dares as the primary source. Elements of Benoît are undoubtedly present (Barnicle points out as many correspondences between the *Seege* and the *Roman de Troie* as with Dares' *Excidio*), and "the romance" referred to on line 197 is clearly the French poem, but of Benoît's additions to the narrative, such as the romance between Jason and Medea, the romance of Troilus and Briseida (Cressida), and Diomedes' defeat of the monstrous "Sagittary", there is no trace.

In defence of Wager, he was at that time assuming the existence of an "enlarged *Roman de Troie*", in an attempt to explain material common to the *Seege of Troye*, the Norse *Trójumanna Saga*, the Bulgarian *Trojanska Prica*, and Konrad von Wurzbürg's *Der Trojanische Krieg* not present in any known manuscript of Benoît, Dares, or Dictys

* Charles Henry Adams Wager (ed.), *The Seege of Troye* (Macmillan, 1899): p. xviii

† Barnicle (1927), p. lvii-lix

‡ A. Zietsch (ed.), "Zwei Mittelenglische Bearbeitungen der Historia de Excidio Trojae des Phrygiers Dares", *Herrig's Archiv*, vol. 72 (1884)

Cretensis. American linguist E. Bagby Atwood put all such speculation to rest in the 1930s with his discovery of the *Rawlinson Excidium Troiae*—the thirteenth-century epitome of a lost Latin work, which provided the "missing link" in the medieval Troy canon.

The *Seege of Troye* survives in four manuscript copies: MSS. Lincoln's Inn 150, Egerton 2862 (formerly Sutherland), Arundel XXII, and Harley 525. Subtle differences in content and phraseology between the four reveal their independence; no one text is the transcript—however corrupt—of another. Rather, each manuscript independently traces its descent from a lost original. Of these, MS. Lincoln's Inn 150 preserves the greatest portion of the original poem, with 1,988 lines out of a probable 2,000 (or thereabouts). Egerton is somewhat shorter at 1,898 lines, and Arundel the shortest at 1,762. Both Lincoln's Inn and Egerton are titled "The Battle of Troy", and this may well have been the poem's original title. MS. Harl. 525 runs to 1,922 lines but is the least faithful of the four, with some parts heavily edited and others—particularly the "battle scenes"—greatly expanded. The Harley version also moves the poem away from its roots as a minstrel romance, with much of the repetition and stock phrasing removed in an attempt to give a more literary veneer. It is later than the others, dating from the middle of the fifteenth century.

At its core, the plot of the *Seege of Troye* is that of Dares Phrygius' *Excidio Trojae Historia* stripped back to its very bones, with the early life of Paris among the herdsmen as well as that of the boy Achilles at the court of King Lycomedes borrowed from the *Rawlinson Excidium Troiae.* The narrative begins with a heavily-truncated quest for the Golden Fleece—now in the possession of the Trojan King Laomedon, which leads to the first destruction of Troy and the abduction of the princess Hesione. This later serves as a pretext for Paris' abduction of Helen—a detail from Dares Phrygius, effectively making the Trojans less culpable for their own demise.

Familiar episodes from the ancient Epic Cycle such as the sacrifice of Iphigenia, the plague of Apollo, and the arrival of the Amazons are passed over, and key characters Diomedes, Deiphobus, Helenus, Cassandra, Calchas, Memnon and Penthesilea disappear entirely. Others, such as Ulysses, Agamemnon, and Palamedes are reduced to mere bit players, with the primary focus being the exploits of Achilles, Hector, Troilus and Paris. Even the legendary wooden horse is nowhere to be seen,* with traitors Antenor and Aeneas agreeing to open the gates for the Greeks in exchange for their lives. The *Seege of Troye* ends with the triumphant Greeks returning home and celebrating their victory with forty days of feasting on "peacocks, pheasants, and bittern" and "venison of hart, and boar" (ll. 1975-6). Of the slew of shipwrecks, assassinations and expulsions which traditionally befell the Greeks upon their homecoming, the poet makes no mention.

Those wishing to read the *Seege of Troye* in the original Middle English are encouraged to seek Mary Elizabeth Barnicle's 1927 edition, which provides a composite of MSS. Lincoln's Inn 150, Egerton 2862 and Arundel XXII, as well as the complete MS. Harl. 525 as an appendix. It is hoped that the present edition—to my knowledge, the first to translate the work into Modern English—will be appreciated by those looking for something rather more accessible than the medieval originals.

I have taken a slightly less aggressive approach to this translation than with the first volume in this series,† allowing more of the archaic, Middle English words to stand—definitions are given in the righthand margin in the first instance, and a glossary is included in Appendix II. Proper names have all been replaced with the Latin or Latinised Greek antecedent except where they must be retained to preserve a rhyme, and a list of the original Middle English spellings and variants may be found in Appendix I. The chapter headings I have largely bor-

* In this the *Seege* poet follows Dares, who does not mention the Trojan Horse.

† D. M Smith (tran.), *A Middle English Iliad: John Lydgate's Troy Book* (Independent, 2018)

rowed from Wager's 1899 edition, with a few of my own—the medieval versions feature no such divisions.

Of the four manuscripts of the *Seege of Troye* I have elected to focus on the Lincoln's Inn and Harleian versions—the former for its apparent fidelity to the original poem, and the latter for its unique digressions.* My initial plan had been to present the two side by side (as per their first official publication in 1884), but I realised early on that translation into Modern English would render vast tracts of them identical. The solution was a composite—the complete text of MS. Lincoln's Inn 150, with MS. Harl. 525's expansions and digressions inserted where appropriate, and any significantly different line readings given in the footnotes. I have stopped short of blending the two manuscripts into an artificial, continuous work: the Harleian additions will instead appear in italics, distinct from the Lincoln's Inn text. The line numbers for each remain independent, respecting those of the original manuscripts.

The Rawlinson Prose Siege of Troy

THE *Rawlinson Prose Siege of Troy* is an unusual document. It exists in a single manuscript copy known as MS. Rawlinson D 82, which also contains a prose summary of Statius' *Thebaid* and an extract from Book VIII of John Gower's *Confessio Amantis*. Its proper title is *The Sege of Troye*, but it is variously known as the "Rawlinson Prose Siege of Troy" or "Rawlinson Prose Troy Piece" to distinguish it from the poem. "Rawlinson" refers to eighteenth-century antiquarian Richard Rawlinson, whose collection of more than five thousand medieval manuscripts was bequeathed to the Bodleian Library at the University of

* The few lines in MSS. Arundel and Egerton that are not present in Lincoln's Inn and Harl. add little of value, although I have inserted one Arundel line to repair an incomplete couplet in the Lincoln's Inn text—this is placed between lines 1523-1524.

Oxford upon his death in 1755 (the *Rawlinson Excidium Troiae* was a part of the same collection). Along with its original title, it shares with the *Seege of Troye* the distinction of being the earliest survivor of its kind—in this case, an English prose history of the Trojan War.

The document was known to scholars in the nineteenth century, but did not appear in print until 1907, when it was published in the Modern Language Association of America journal *PMLA* by Nathaniel Edward Griffin.[*] It has received little attention since then, and its origins and purpose are a mystery, although Griffin identified a Southern dialect of the fifteenth century.

In the opening line the author cites "the noble and worthy clerk Guido" and "the famous clerk Dares" as his sources, and for many years this appears to have gone unchallenged. Early descriptions of the text as "a prose adaptation of Guido's *Historia*"[†] probably assumed the reference to Dares Phrygius was merely parroting Guido's, but Griffin noted several details and phrasings which had indeed come directly from Dares rather than via the Sicilian. His opinion was that the work was not a direct translation or redaction from the Latin, but rather "an intermediary French version", based on "the frequent employment of Gallicisms in the English text".[‡] At the time of writing, Henry Bergen's edition of Lydgate's *Troy Book* was still being prepared for publication; had this been available to him, Griffin would have quickly identified *Troy Book* as the intermediary. Certain Anglicisations of the Latin names in the *Rawlinson Prose Siege* and *Troy Book* are nearly identical, and material identified by Griffin as extrinsic to Guido's *Historia*—such as Ganymede and Polydorus being sons of Priam,[§] and Jason abandoning Medea for another wife—are readily found in Lydgate. As

[*] Nathaniel Edward Griffin, "The Sege of Troye", *PMLA* vol. 22, no. 1 (1907): pp. 157-200

[†] H. Oskar Sommer (ed.), *The Recuyell of the Historyes of Troye* vol. 1 (David Nutt, 1894): p. xliv

[‡] Griffin (1907), p. 172

[§] Ganymede was traditionally the son of Tros, the first King of Troy.

for his supposed Gallic words and phrases, enough of these appear in *Troy Book* that they may be quietly dismissed as a red herring.

The author's dependence on Lydgate was noted by Friedrich Brie in 1913 when he republished the *Rawlinson Prose Siege* in *Herrig's Archiv*. He also believed the redaction of the *Thebaid* in the same manuscript to derive from Lydgate's *Siege of Thebes*.*

The narrative is heavily compressed, but unevenly so—the "Golden Fleece" portion (which equates to Lydgate's Book I) occupies well over a third of the text, and is told in great detail with a particular focus on the romance of Jason and Medea. As the story goes on events become more and more condensed—as though the author was steadily losing patience; had they maintained the same level of detail with which they began, it would have resulted in a document three or four times the size. The Trojan War narrative itself is somewhat garbled, with numerous inaccuracies when set against its probable sources—such as a host of Trojan leaders appended to the list of Greeks who assembled to recover Helen, and Antenor being slain by Aeneas. Griffin's theory is that the author "read large sections ... at a time and then reproduced them from memory."†

In terms of plot, the *Rawlinson Prose Siege of Troy* essentially reproduces Lydgate's *Troy Book*, albeit heavily redacted and reduced to the dimensions of Dares' *Excidio*—that is, ending with the fall of the city. Thus all of Lydgate's Book V is omitted, with the apology that "it would make a long process" to describe the misadventures of the returning Greeks. Anything not immediately pertinent to the wider narrative has been excised: the Greek invasion of Mysia, the romance of Troilus and Cressida, the brief tenure of Palamedes as commander-in-chief, the arrival of the Amazons and the death of their queen, as well as numerous other subplots and incidental episodes.

* Friedrich Brie (ed.), "Zwei Mittelenglische Prosaromane: The Sege of Thebes und The Sege of Troy", *Herrig's Archiv*, vol. 130 (1913): p. 45

† Griffin (1907), p. 164

The Middle English text of the *Rawlinson Prose Siege of Troy* is still basically readable (provided one has the patience!), and both Griffin's 1907 edition and Brie's 1913 transcript of the entire MS. Rawlinson D 82 may be found online. It has never—as far as I am aware—appeared in modern English. For this translation I have primarily relied on Griffin as my foundation, accepting his punctuation and separation into paragraphs for the most part; in many instances I have gone much further, the original's interminable run-on sentences and propensity for anacoluthon requiring some careful editing and liberal use of the comma, full stop, dash and semi-colon to make it decipherable.

I have also borrowed the 1907 chapter headings—the original manuscript does not contain chapters. The definitions of those Middle English words which I could not (or chose not to) translate appear in the glossary in Appendix I. As with the *Seege of Troye* I have changed all proper names to the Latin versions, with the Middle English originals recorded in Appendix II

THE SEEGE OF TROYE

THE SEEGE OF TROYE

Translated from the Lincoln's Inn MS. 150, with supplementary passages from the Harley MS. 525

How Jason undertook the Quest of the Golden Fleece

SINCE God had this world wrought,
Heaven and earth and all of naught,
Many adventures have befall
That we know of them naught all;
Therefore I will a moment dwell
And the Battle of Troy tell.
For such a battle as it was one,
Certainly I know of none;
Thirty winters without fail*
Men of Greece held great battle
With the King of Troy, stout and grim,
And at the last they o'ercame him.
So said a knight that there was,
That was callèd Sir Dares;
He saw that war, without fail,
And did write that same battle.[1]
And such a master of subtle engine
Turned it from Greek into Latin;
And out of Latin, well I wot, *know*

* Harl. 525: "Two and thirty winters, without fail"

A clerk in English thus it wrote.
    My lords, in Greece a man there was;
A prince that hight Sir Pelias.
He was not of Greece highest lording,
For o'er him was a higher king.[2]
He was called Prince of Pelpenson, *Peloponnese*
And had a nephew that hight Jason. *was named*
Jason was fair, for the nonce;
Stiff and strong of body and bones.
Courteous and hende, hardy and bold; *gracious*
All folk him loved, both young and old.
The king called to him Sir Jason,
And gave unto him this reason:
"I am made," he said, "to understand,
That the King of Troy hath in his land
The quaintest thing above mold: *above ground*
That is a sheep's skin of gold.
Might'st thou with thy quaintest gin *trickery; guile*
From the king that sheep's skin win,
And bring to me that skin of gold,
Thy travail acquit ye well I would."[3] *reward*
    "By my faith," said Jason then,
"I shall do all that I can.
To the Trojans I shall fare,
Tidings for to spy there.
But if I may with any gin,
Bring I shall that sheep's skin."
    When the king heard he would go,
He sent for wrights, many one,
And bade they should timber take,
And a secure ship for Jason make.
The king did make a secure ship
That stood above the water deep,

And it was both stiff and good;
The mast was gold therein stood.
And when it was all ready wrought,
And was on the water brought,
He did it charge without fail
With meat and drink, and other victuals.
He also provisioned corn and hay,
To steeds and to palfreys;
So it was thus victualled.
He took with him knights armèd well;
He took with him Sir Hercules,
That stalwart knight and hardy was,
And many another, hardy and hende, *ready*
With him for to Troy to wend.
The knights shipped with game and play,
And sailed forth both night and day,
That o'er the sea the wind them drives,
And up at Troy they arrive.
They made their ship at haven stand;
Hercules and Jason went to land.[4]

How King Laomedon warned the Greeks out of his dominions

THE King of Troy, Sir Laomedon
—Who was a wondrous wise man—
Heard tell that men of Greece were come,
Into his land, all and some.
The king commanded, "Turn again,
Or they shall die, knight and swain!" *squire*
And swore also, must he thrive,
Aliens should not on his land arrive,
And commanded them to turn again,

Or they should die, both knight and swain.
Sir Hercules and Jason both,
That thither were come to that scathe *harm; misfortune*
Of his words aggrievèd were,
And o'er the king ashamèd sore;
To be so rebukèd of a king
So as they had mis-done no thing.
To dwell there longer they thought no good,
And sailed again over the flood,
And passèd forth, naught to lain,
And home to Greece they came again.[5]
Before four barons they have gone;
Great lordings they were each one.
The one was Pollux, the other Castor,
The third Telamon, the fourth Nestor.
"My lord!" they said, "hear beginning and end,
How the King of Troy us did shend! *shame*
And lest his words be dear abought,
Each one of us is told for naught.
Therefore help with your succour,
And maintain our own honour;
Else men of Troy that be stout and fierce
Will hold us all for losengers." *deceivers; cowards*
So spake Sir Pollux and Sir Castor,
Sir Telamon and Sir Nestor,
And swore all in a company,
And said they would, all stoutly,
Amongst the Trojans come and gone
To grieve the king, Sir Laomedon.
"And maugre him and all of his, *in spite of*
We will do all that good is.
Now go we all manly about,
And gather us a noble rout;

Upon his land we will arrive,
And look who will us thence drive!"
They did make ships, money and gold,
For to passen o'er the flood,
And chargèd them, well and sure,
And victualled them with good armour.
They took with them great chivalry
And went to ship full hastily,
And drawing sail the wind was good,
And sailed them o'er the salty flood.
All by water did they wend,
And at Troia did they land.
They arrivèd all on land,
Of adventures for to find.
The city folk wondered what they'd do,
Whither they came, and where to.
In the city was much folk speaking
—And many a man ill looking—
And made the king to understand
That ships of Greece were come to land
With many folk, stout and grim,
And said they would besiegen him.

Of the First Destruction of Troy, and how King Laomedon was slain by Hercules

THE king anon did make a cry:
All folk should arm them hastily,
And them dight themselves well— *furnish; equip*
Both in iron and in steel.
And all that might bear a brand
Or any weapon in his hand,

With arbalest or with bow bent: *crossbow*
This was the king's commandèment.
The king him armèd anon right,
And all his folk was well dight, *well equipped*
And went hastily out of the town
And came together upon a down.
And when they were together met,
There were strokes well a-set;
There was cracked many a crown,
And many stout bachelor fell a-down.

There might men see shafts a-shake,
And many crowns all to-crack.
There were shields gilt and laid with ind, *indigo*
And banners rustled with the wind.
Many noble men under shield
Soon were slain in that field.

The King of Troy with Hercules met
And gave him strokes well a-set.
And Hercules, with his might,
Defended as a hardy knight,
So that within a little stound *moment*
The King of Troy was brought to ground.

The king with Hercules hath met,
And hard strokes on him set,
And with a lance smote him there,
That from his saddle he did him bear.
Sir Hercules, for that dint,
Fell down on the pavèment.[6]
Then came riding Sir Jason

With a lance to Laomedon;
Hard together there they drives,
That their shafts all to-rives.
Swords they drawen in that stound,
And each gave other grisly wound;
And strong battle there began
Betwixt Sir Jason and Laomedon.
There while the pair did fight
There came of Greece two hundred knights,
And brought on horse Sir Hercules—
All enarmèd as he was.
And when he was upon his steed
He thought he burned as any glede;
With a lance he came forth then,
Riding to Sir Laomedon

He struck the king through the sides too;
Three of his sons he did also.[7]
The men of Troy in a little stound
The Grecians brought them all to ground.
When the king to death did fall
Hercules and his fellows all
Went and robbed that rich city;
Of men nor women had no pity.
The king had no daughters but one,
And she was hight Dame Hesione.
When she heard her father had lost his life
She has gone and hid herself,
And Hercules that was so stout,
Full hastily he found her out,
And led her to ship in by—
No wonder then she were sorry!

She had sorrow and much thought,
For her father was to death brought;
Her three brethren and all her kin—
Great was the sorrow she was in.
Hercules won the skin also, *the Golden Fleece*
For which was wakened all this woe.
They took treasure, armour also,
And then in haste to ship did go,
And passèd o'er the salty foam.
And to Greece they comen home,
And made merry and slew care,
And looked how they best might fare.
The former battle this then was
Wherethrough were many fatherless.
The war did last, I understand,
Thirty winters with much wrong.
The babes in mothers' wombs that were
Waxed and 'venged their fathers there.
Thus was the king then brought to ground
With dint of sword and spear's wound;
His barons and all his chivalry,
Burgesses and bachelors of that city.
So saith the romance, I understand,
Hercules took the princess by the hand
And brought her to Greece with much care,
And looked how they best might fare.[8]
But forsooth, they knew naught all *indeed*
After that mirth what would befall.
Stint we now of all that joy,
And speak we of the King of Troy.
I tell you all, without fail,
Thus ended the First Battle.

Of the lamentation of Priam and the dream of Hecuba

LISTEN my lords, ere ye gang, *before you go*
Of the King of Troy that was dead with wrong:
He had a son that Priamus hight,
That was a man of mickle might; *much*
Through heritage to him would fall
To be the King of Trojans all.
In the land of Phrygia he was that time
With child and wife we find in rhyme,
And of that discomfit knew he naught;
How his father was to death brought,
And his three brethren on that day,
And his fair sister led away.[9]
He said, "Alas! Who hath done that deed?
Of friends am I now full in need
Now that Troy is thus destroyed!"
He sorrowed and was sore annoyed.

"Alas, who hath my father slain,
And my brothers brought a-down,
And ravished my sister, Dame Hesione?
Alas! Now friends have I none!"

King Priamus had sons three:
Noble men, courteous and free.
Sir Hector was his eldest son, iwis, *for certain*
Troilus, and Alexander Paris.[10]
The night Alexander was got of man *begotten*
A dream his mother dreamèd then:
That from her body a branch sprang,
That burnèd Troy and all that land.
And when she woke of her dreaming,

She sent for masters, old and young,
And when they were all a-come
Before the queen, all and some,
She told her dream before them all
And bade them say what should befall;
And bade them say and nothing lie,
What her dream should signify.
"Madame," they said, "without lies,
In thy body a child there is
That shall bring Troy all to naught:
For him many men to death be brought."
For this the queen was full of woe,
And said to them, "It shall not be so!"
When the child was born of that lady,
Fairer might no man see with eye.
Nurses many to him were sought;
The child attended fair and soft.
And when the child was seven years old
He was fair and of speech bold;
His mother thought on her dreaming
That she met in her sleeping,
And thought that he should slay no men,
Nor the city of Troy make be slain.
She made the child's clothing tight
—Kirtle and tabard and hood all white—
And made him to the fields to go
To keep swine with staff and stone,
Under a man that better couth *could*
That knew the fields by north and south.
The queen sent her own child
Into a country waste and wild,
And made him keep swine there
As if he a poor man's son were.[11]

For he ne'er should see no armour bright,
Nor any battle, nor any fight.

There he was out of knowing,
Years fifteen, without lying.[12]

But when the child saw fight bull or boar
Or other beast, less or more,
He had great joy them to behold
Which of them other o'ercome should.
The child would cause the beasts to fight,
And had great joy of that sight;
And which beast would fight and stand
He would him crown with a garland.[13]
Of all deeds the child was wise,
Therefore the child was called Paris.[14]

Of the rebuilding of Troy

THE king his father heard the saw *saying; speech*
How his son was wise of law,
And after the child did he send
With him to Troia for to wend.
His queen, his son, with him he named,
And hastily to Troy he came
And swore and said all of his thought:
His father's death should be dear a-bought.
And after masons he sent anon
That well could work with lime and stone;
And go to work they did all,
The city of Troy to be-wall.

Verily, without ween, doubt
There was no mason in that realm
Would take a drachm of gold a day
But that they might fetch there their pay.

They made the walls wondrous high—
Fairer man might ne'er espy.
The city he closèd with a ditch—
No deeper under heaven rich.
And seven gates he made, iwis,
With drawbridge and portcullis.
And when the sea was high in flood
It ran about the city good.

The ditch was so roomy and large,
Therein might sail both boat and barge.
Great ships in there might row;
There was joy and mirth enough.

And when it ebbèd againward, back again
The ditch should be deep and hard

That no man ne'er enter may
Against their will, sooth to say. truth

A better city was ne'er under sun;
For certain it might ne'er be won
Unless that it were through treason.
In all the world was ne'er such town.
And in Troy he made a tower:
Of all towers it was flower.
And in the tower he made an altar,

Of the false god, Sir Jupiter;
A mammet rich for the nonce, *idol*
Of gold, silver, and precious stones
(This was many hundred years before
Jesus were of Mary born—
They ne'er knew other avowry
But false gods and mammetry).
In that tower Priam made his dwelling;
A richer never had no king.
When the tower was dight as it be shall
Priam sent for his barons all,
And did crown him king anon—
And Hecuba his queen also.
Hector his eldest son he tas; *takes*
A prince under him he was.
His other son, Alexander Paris
—That was held aware and wise—
An earldom succeeded in his hand;
His friends he made lords of his land.
And since he made his parliament,
And after all his kingdom sent,
When the parliament plenar was *full; complete*
The same man said his advice:

Of the parliament of the Trojans and the embassy of Antenor

"FIRSTLY then," said Priamus,
And said, "My lords, thus and thus,
Ye wit how Grecians hither come
And this land they slew and nome, *took*
And our friends they have destroyed—
All ye ought to be annoyed.

If ye will hereto counsel,
I shall them give a new battle,
And war on them both night and day!"
    And his council said, "Sir, nay!
Better were peace fore'er and whole
Than battle, slaughter, war and woe.
We rede you do as king hende, *advise*
Some wise barons hither to send
To them that our elders slew
And our goods away drew.
And if they will amends doen,
For all that they did in this town,
And send again thy sister bright
—Dame Hesione, fair of sight—
If they will do so, good is;
And if they won't, do your advice."
    The king said, "I grant thereto
Who may best the message do."
Among them all they said the one
Sir Antenor must therefore go.[15]
Antenor granted and graithèd him *made ready*
And passed the sea that was so grim,
And took with him what he would also,
And drew sail and forth did go.
Night and day forth did they ride,
And came to Greece with mickle pride.
The messenger came to Hercules
—That master of that discomfit was—[*]
And to Sir Pollux and Sir Castor,
Sir Telamon and Sir Nestor,
And said to them, "I am come here

[*] Harl. 525: "That master over Africa was"

From Troia as a messenger.
King Priam made me hither wend
To wit if that ye will amend
Of this thing: ye came against the peace
And slew his father, guilty-less.
And which of ye hath his sister hende,
I rede that he again her send.
For certainly it is un-right:
A king's daughter to serve a poor knight.
Therefore I rede thou to him go
And do in his mercy anon."
    Now to him spake a great lording—
Full sorely him liked that tiding.
Hercules was his name called:
He was a baron mighty bold.
"Fie on devils!" said Hercules,
"Such despite to us ne'er was!
Should we in his mercy abide?
Nay, that shall us ne'er betide.
Go tell your king he did us wrong—
We him another also strong.
And if thou were no messenger,
Full evil hadst thou come to here!
And if thou think'st to pass alive,
Truss thee hence, and that swithe!" *promptly*

How the Trojans prepared to make war upon the Greeks

ANTENOR saw it was no bote *benefit*
Against them all for to moot, *debate*
And turned again without tarrying
And came home and told Priam the King.

He hath told the king his lord
How he was rebuked, every word.
The king was so wondrously wroth,
And swore many a hard oath
That he should never be blithe
'Til he were 'vengèd, and that swithe.
He sent about swiftly anon
After shipwrights, many one,
And bade them go and timber take
And four score ships them to make.[*]
And when that they were all wrought
And upon the water brought,
He chargèd them, without fail,
With meat and drink and other victuals;
Both provisioned with corn and hay,
To steeds, coursers, and palfrey.
The king purveyed through counsel
A noble host without rascal.

When they were gathered with great hying *haste*
They came to Troy before the king.
The king thought no longer to land,
But dight them forth ready to wend.

He made them bound to Greece to fare
With all his knights, less and more.
Now came Hector, his son eldest
—Of all his brethren he was boldest—
And said thus to his lord the king:
"I rede thou go to Greece no thing,
But dwell at home and merry make,

[*] Harl. 525: "And felleth timber and 'gan to hew / And forty ships he did make new"

And thine host I will take
And war against our enemies,
And stoutly bring thee home the prize."
    The king answered with words still:
"I allow son thy good will."
Priam hoped he would be a good warrior
And granted him all his power,
And bade him take his host anon
And go avenge him on his foe.

Of the Judgement of Paris

THEN came forth Alexander Paris
—The king's middlest son of prize—
And said thus to his lord the king:
"I shall you tell another thing:
If ye take yourself your host,
And wendest thither with mickle boast,
Ye may be discomfited and overthrown,
And your folk slain—every one.
Yet Sire, will ye hear another:
If ye send forth Hector my brother,
His host and he may be all to-torn,
And then we will all be forlorn.
I rede that ye dwell still here
And let me go forth with your power,
And I shall in Greece war so
That men shall speak thereof e'er more,
And win the mastery with much honour,
And come again as conqueror."
    Then answered Priamus the King,
And said unto his son young:

"Son," he said, "how speak'st thou now?
Hector is ten times strong as thou!
Thou tell me, I command thee,
How hopest thou to speed better than he?"
"Sire," he said then, "truly,
I wot it well, certainly.
Hearken, Father, to my spell,
And of a wonder I shall thee tell:
This other day I went in the forest
To hunt and take some wild beast;
I took the hunters and hounds ten
To witten how they would run.
We had mickle game and glee;
Of venison had great plenty.
Now went we each one our way far
To hunt for the wild deer.
I pricked and rode forth at good pace;
The weather changed—great mist there was—
So that I lost my fellows each one;
Of all them saw I not one.
And in the forest I rode so long
That my right way I lost, and took the wrong.
So within a little while
I passed into the forest two mile;
Anon a sleep then I took,
That I ne'er might ride nor look.
I alighted down upon the ground
And lay and slept a little stound.
And as I slept under that tree,
Dear Father, listen to me:
In that forest were gangand *going*
Four ladies of Elven-Land.[16]
That time of them wist I no deal, *I knew nothing*

But afterward I wist well.
And as they wenten them to play,
They found a ball of gold, verily.
It was a fully rich ball:
Of burnished gold it was all.
Thereon was all in letters
—Letters of silver—full fair scripture
That some clerk might it read
That to book was set, or scholar good.
The letters said: '*The fairest woman of all*
Shall have and wield this rich ball.'[17]
"Saturnus the eldest the ball up-took,
And on the letters did she look,
And said, 'I will have this rich ball,
And when me liketh play withal.'
"'Nay,' said Jupiter, 'God me save,
This rich ball I will have.
For I am fairer, so have I bliss;
So am I held where wise men is.'
"'Nay,' said Mercurius, "so must I go:
I am fairer than thee both.
Therefore I will have this rich ball,
And when me liketh play withal.'
"Then spoke Venus full hendely,
'Sisters, quarrel cannot I,
But there,' she said, 'layeth a knight—
He shall try all our right;
Which of us shall have the ball.'
And thereto granted these sisters all.
"Father," said Paris, "thus it was.
Hear now a wondrous case:
Then have these women to me gone,
And stood before me, every one,

And bade me anon rise up and wake
And in mine hand the ball to take,
And give the ball there courteously
As the letters spake, to the fairest lady.
Which was the fairest I could not sayen;
They were so fair, every one.
Then spake Saturnus to me full soon:
"'Knight, give me the ball and have done.
A better gift I will give thee
If thou the ball will give to me:
I shall thee make the richest man
That livèd under God alone.
For I have might to give riches
To whom I will, more and less;
Therefore this ball give thou to me,
And great riches I shall give thee.
What kind of riches thou wilt crave,
For the ball shalt thou have.'
"And I thought I was rich enough now—
What should I with more riches do?
"Then spake Mercurius, that other lady:
'Knight, give me the ball for thy courtesy,
And I shall give thee strength and might:
In all the world shall be no such knight.
Hector nor no knight in the land
Shall have no might against thy hand.
In tournament nor battle, far nor near,
In all this world shall have no peer.
For I have power to give men might—
Both to squire and to knight.
Therefore this fair ball give thou me,
And much strength I shall give thee.'
"I thought I was strong enough now—

What should I with more strength do?
"Then said Jupiter, the third lady:
'Knight, give me the ball for thy courtesy
And thou shalt be the fairest man
That livèd under God alone.
For of beauty I have the might
To make both fair, clerk and knight.
Therefore give the ball to me
And a fair knight I shall make thee.'
"And I thought I was fair enough now—
What should I with more beauty do?
"So spake Venus the fourth lady:
'Knight, give me the ball for thy courtesy
And thou shalt have love and would;
All folk shall love thee, young and old.
All women that thee see with sight
Shall thee love with all their might.
Maidens in chamber shall love thee all;
Ladies in bower and wives in hall.
All women shall be in thy poustie, *power*
And all thereafter shall love thee.'
"Then had I much of bliss
To have the love of all of this,
And gave her the ball hastily,
And said she was the fairest lady.
And I said then, mote I thee, *might I thrive (an oath)*
She was fairer than the three
In all things, truly."

"Sir," he said, "listen a stound:
Three goddesses an apple found
—Juno, the Lady of Wiseness,
Dame Pallas, and Dame Venus—

That Fortune cast, without lies,
To maken war that ere was peace.
That apple was with gold engraved
And said the fairest it should have.
Then said Juno, 'Mine shall it be,
For I am fairest of us three.'[18]
"Pallas said, 'It shall be mine'
—She swore by Jupiter and Apolline— Apollo
'For well 'tis known and understand:
Fairest I am in any land.'
"Dame Venus said, 'Now ye be still:
That apple is mine by right skill.
For I am, without lies,
The fairest ever born that was.'
"Dame Juno said, 'By Mohammed, nay.[19]
In no wise it may not be
That it be at our judgement,
For each sees her own talent.'
"'Thou sayest sooth,' said Pallas, 'surely
Another man that must decree
Which of us shall have this jewel.'
"Then said Venus, 'Thou sayest well.
Paris is the truest man
That ever God laid life upon;
Best it is that our judge he be,
Who shall have it of us three.'
"They all granted thereto, iwis.
Juno she went unto Paris,
And said, 'Paris, wilt thou be,
For great need I come to thee.
For an apple that we found

Early this day upon the ground;
That apple Paris thou me give,
Thou shalt be wise while thou may live.'
"Paris said, 'So I will,
If thou have thereto skill.'
"Pallas the way from him has taken,[20]
And Venus to him was comen,
And said, 'Paris, well be thou, aye,
Mohammed thee save that best may.
For thou art the truest knight,
And all things thou judgest right.
Therefore, Paris, I pray thee
This apple that thou grant to me
That we found this other day,
As we went on in our play.
That apple, Paris, grant thou me:
A fair leman I will give thee; lover
Thou shalt have the fairest leman
That ever God laid life upon.'
"And then Sire, I bethought me so
That Juno had no right thereto;
Though she were Lady of Wiseness,
She had not so much fairness.
Nor Pallas, Sir, so mote I thee;
Venus was fairer than she.
Therefore I granted her to have
The apple that was with gold engrave.
And therefore, with mine intent,
Thus I gave the judgèment."

"And Venus said, well hendely,
'Alexander I shall quit thee
That thou hast thus honoured me.
Bid thy father as he is king hende:
Grant thee unto Greece to wend.
For nothing shalt thou there dread—
Full well shalt thou thereto speed.
The fairest lady that beareth life
Thou shalt wed unto thy wife.'
"Therefore Sire, let me thither wend."
His father granted as king hende.

Sir Hector and his brethren all
Answered Priam in his hall,
And said, "If Alexander Paris
Goes to Troy to win the prize,
The men of Greece will stint no stound
Ere that Troy be brought to ground."
Nevertheless, the king anon
Granted Paris for to go.

And all his power him betakes,
And master o'er his host him makes,
And bade him bear himself manly
And o'er all things steer him stoutly;
And ever more with all his might
Maintain well his father's right.

How Alexander deceived the Greeks as to the purpose of his voyage

ALEXANDER and his folk each one
In haste did them to ship be gone.
Then was Alexander full of jollity
Sailing the sea with royal company,
With four score ships, good and strong.*
The masts of fir were good and long;
Each mast had fane of red sendal *a banner of red silk*
With the sign of Troy wrought full well,
And with new sails of cloth,
And had good wind, and forth they goeth.
Night and day forth they drive,
And come to Greece and there arrive.
The city folk wondered what they'd do,
And whence they came, and where to.
Many came them to behold,
And hendely asked what they would.
Alexander Paris and all of his
Answered now with words wise:

"Merchants," he said. "That we be;
Out of the Ottoman Sea come we,
And a tempest hither us drove.
Therefore, my lords, be not wroth.
We ne'er dwell but a day or two,
Then we will take leave and go;
And perhaps it may betide,
We will not so long abide."

* Harl. 525: "With forty ships good and strong"

And learned whereabout to spy and hear
In what country Hercules were,
And Sir Pollux and Sir Castor,
Telamon and Sir Nestor,
And all the lords every one
That took his aunt, Dame Hesione.
They thought on much and said naught ill,
But aye they hoped to have their will.
So it befell in that time
—As we finden in our rhyme—
The High King of Greece, Sir Menelae *Menelaus*
Sojournèd both night and day
In that very court and all,
With a main well royal *retinue*

In one of the noblest cities
That was in all that country.
It was called Cytherion; *Cythera*
In all the world was no such town—
Save for Troy, trusty and true,
For that was lately builded new.
Solomon the Conqueror,
Nor David of more honour, *Kings of Israel*
Nor the King Alexander *Alexander the Great*
—Of whom there was so great slander—
Held not so royal a main
As Menelaus in his domain.[21]

He was both king and emperor,
And reigned in Greece with much honour,
And had with him Dame Helen, his queen;
She that was both bright and sheen.

A fairer creature that was one
Before her was never none.
She was gentle, courteous and free—
All folk her loved in that country.

> *Fairer formed was never one*
> *In all this world, both blood and bone;*
> *She was full of goodliness,*
> *Might no man tellen her fairness—*
> *Virgil, though alive he were,*
> *Or Aristotle that could more,*
> *Or Nectanebo, that noble clerk,*
> *That could most of such work,*
> *To describe woman's fairness,*
> *Her beauty, and her meekness;*
> *Dame Olympias, I understand,*
> *Crownèd him with a garland,*
> *O'er all masters to bear the prize,*
> *For that he was so good and wise.*[22]

Sir Menelaus of Greece the King
Heard tell of that new tiding;
Of Sir Alexander Paris.
The King of Troy's son comen is
Into his land with great chivalry,
But he ne'er wist wherefore nor why.[23]

Of the Rape of Helen, and the Second Battle

HELEN the Queen with blissful mood
Spake more words than were good,
And began to say thus and thus:
"Much folk speak of Priamus,
That King of Troy crownèd is,
And of his son Alexander Paris
That come is hither with strength and might.
Men tell he is a fair knight,
And therefore," she said, "so mote I thee,
Me longeth sore him to see.
Never shall I blithe be,
'Til I him may with eyen see."
    A squire heard that tiding well,
And told Sir Alexander all.
"By my faith," said Paris, "I do also,
To see her eye and visage too.
Blithe now will I never be
'Til I may her with eyen see."
    Upon a day Helen the Queen,
With knights and pretty ladies ten,
Came to a temple with much bliss.
And Sir Alexander heard tell this,
And graithed him with great chivalry,
And came to the temple hastily;
Without which they can meet,
And hendely each the other greet.
Each beheld other lovingly;
Both were fair and comèly.
The queen beheld Alexander oft,
And in her heart so she thought
That she ne'er saw a fairer knight

—Neither by day, nor by night—
And thought her heart would to spring,
So was she caught in love longing.
    Paris saw the queen forth go,
And sorely sicked, and was full woe;
The love of her had took so blive, *swiftly*
That nigh his heart did break in five.
He said he would not eat no meat,
Ere he her with strength could get;
And to his host made to be gone,
And had them arm them, every one,
And commanded his men arm him,
And his weapon with him nome,
And first said of all things:
"Take Sir Menelaus the King,
And where that e'er the king be come,
That the queen be also nome. *seized*
And each man force him well to do,
And I myself shall do also."

Now every man forth they shove
For Alexander their lord's love.

    Then Paris rode forth with his host,
Crying and blowing with much boast;
Fast assault did they begin,
The city the king and queen were in.
On each side the Trojan vessels all
Gave assault unto the wall;
Each mast had a top castle,
And assailed the city hard and well,
And began stones to shoot and cast.
The city folk defended fast;

Paris lost many of his men,
With shot of bow and dint of stone.
Many good body he felled a-down,
And defended as a noble baron;
Helms a-riven and shields rapped,
And many head from body swapped.
There was no baron, knight nor swain,
That might withstand this dint against.
No wall or gate about the town
He and his host ne'er felled a-down.
Paris and his folk slew that day
Folk that no man number may.
The King of Greece saw his knights all
Were slain, and to ground were fall,
And was a-dread to go to death,
And fled away and forth he goeth
So no man wist where he became.

Of Alexander's return to Troy, and the lamentation of Helen

AND Paris to the queen hath nome
And took the queen in her weed,
And set her before him on his steed
—The queen grieved and made great cry—
And led her forth to ship in hie; *in haste*
And many countesses and ladies too—
The fairest that on earth might go.
Therewhile his folk robbed and reaved;
In all that country naught they leaved.
With treasure they chargèd their ships well;
The treasure they took like a deal. *in the same way*
Longer to dwell they were loath,

Avoiding the land for doubt of scathe.
Paris came home to his father's tower;
His father welcomed him with honour,
And said, "How hast thou sped, son mine?"
"Father," he said, "well and fine.
I have destroyed in all things,
Of all Greece the great lordings.
The king himself, Sir Menelae,
Away is fled, well away.
The queen I have, white as flour,
With all the maidens of her bower.
The gold, the silver, great and small,
And treasure of that country all."
The King of Troy laughèd so,
For he hath so well a-done.
But Dame Helen weepeth sore,
And all the ladies that with her were.
"In heart," she said, "me is full woe!
Why not will it burst a-two?

"Alas alas that I was born!"
She wept and wrung ever more.
Her hair that shineth as gold wire,
She to-drew, and her noble attire.

"Alas, why won't my heart to-rive?
All too long am I alive!"
Alexander, that good knight,
Comforted her with all his might,
And loved her as his own life,
And her wedded to his wife.
First she was queen and empress,
And now but a simple countess.

Paris had at his wedding
Of that land every lording,
And held a feast swithe royal *very*
As every king's son shall.
There was joy and melody,
Of all skins minstrelry
Of trumpets, tuber, harp and crouth, *a stringed instrument*
And many merry disour of mouth. *storyteller*
They were given gifts for the nonce
Of gold, silver, and precious stones.
The more merry that these men made,
The more sorrow Dame Helen had.
They that were there wist not all
After that mirth what would befall.
But rest we now a little piece,
And speak we of the King of Greece.
So my lords, without fail,
Thus can end the Second Battle.

Of the lamentation of King Menelaus for the ravishing of his wife, and the marshalling of the Greeks

THE King of Greece, Sir Menelae,
Sickened and sorrowed night and day,
And with much sorrow led his life,
And sore bemoaned Helen his wife.

666 *Her beauty and her fairness,*
Her gentle body, her loveliness.

"Alas!" he said, "my wife is ta'en,
My earls and barons all are slain,

And all my land robbed and reaved,
And I myself in sorrow leaved!"
And when he saw he might no other,
He sent anon after his brother
That was called Agamemnon;
He was a duke, a noble man,
And also sent for Sir Dares;[24]
The best knight that in his land was.
Agamemnon and Dares in all things
Solaced and comforted their king,
And bade the king to send wide
O'er all his kingdom on each side
To all men that were of eld—
Any that might weapon wield,
Should come before him every one;
The king granted thereto anon.
He sent anon without dwelling
Overall to each lording;
To duke and earl, baron and knight,
And to each man that was of might,

That every one of them should bring
To him their power in all things;
Of good ships, great and wide—
For all by water they must ride.

And be gathered on their side
All men that might go or ride
And comen to a certain stead;
And so every lording did.
The King of Greece, without lies,
A little mean man he was. *moderate*
His head was red, his beard also;

The hendest knight that e'er might go.
He was stalwart and hardy among,
And him was loath to suffer wrong.[25]
    The king purveyed with all his might
A great host, and well dight.
The king did make ships five hundred*
—So much it were that it was wonder—
And did them charge, without fail,
With meat and drink and good victuals;
Some provisioned with corn and hay,
To steeds and to palfreys.
The king gathered a full-good rout
Of strong men, and of stout.

The Catalogue of Ships [26]

THE king's brother, Agamemnon,
Was a wondrous mickle man; *large or great*

706 *Fair of body, quaint, and rich;*
He was not his brother like.

He was Duke of Mycenae,
And brought with him ships fifty,
And a host stout and good
To pass over the salty flood.
    Sir Dares came full well dight;
In arms he was a doughty knight.
A hardier man bore never bones;
Courteous and large for the nonce.

* Harl. 525: "And maked him ships a hundred"

Glad of semblance and ruddy;
A lord he was of Parchy. *Sparta*
He brought fifty ships, good and sure,
Furnished well with good armour,
And a host stout and good
To pass over the salty flood.
Polypoetes of Thessaly;
Four score ships he brought him by,
And a host stout and good
To pass over the salty flood.
Sir Nestor, the Lord of Pyle, *Pylos*
He brought with him out of his isle
A great host and a well cure, *well chosen*
And good ships there were, four score.
Sir Podarces of Phylacè,
Brought ships four and thirty,
And a host stout and good
To passen o'er the salty flood.
Arcesilaus the Lord of Boise, *Boeotia*
Of all his land he brought the choice
Of good men and hardy,
And brought with him ships fifty.
Guneus of Cyphus also
Brought twenty ships and no more,
With many stout bachelor,
And went therefore with glad cheer.
The warrior Ascalaphus,
He was lord of Orchomenus;
Thirty ships he brought with him,
And a host stout and grim.

And also Patroclus the lord,
With warriors stout and good;

Forty ships he brought in hie,
With well-fair chivalry.
Polyxenus and Telamon
That lords were of Anthedon,[27]
Brought good ships of defence,
With their victuals and their dispense;
Four score ships upon the flood,
And wight men in armour good. — *strong*

Sir Prothous of Magnesie — *Magnesia*
Brought with him vessels forty,
And a host stout and good
To passen o'er the salty flood.
Epistrophus of Paladide, — *Phocis*
He brought his host him beside,
Armèd well unto the teeth,
And forty ships also he doth.
Menestheus of Athenè — *Athens*
Brought with him ships full fifty,
And a host with much joy
To wend with the king to Troy.
Sir Ajax of Salamain — *Salamis*
Brought his host with might and main,
And forty ships, good and sure,
Victualled with good armour. — *equipped*
Agapenor of Arcadie — *Arcadia*
Brought with him vessels forty,
And a host stout and gay
With all the joy that he may.
Sir Podalirius as well,
With his lord went he well,
And brought his host with strength and might

And twenty ships, well a-dight.
Philoctetes of Meliboea;
Seven ships he brought, and no more,
And came to Greece as I thou say — *as I tell you*
Where the greater navy lay.
Sir Thoas of Aetolie — *Aetolia*
Brought strong ships three and thirty,
And a host stout and good
To pass over the salty flood.
Sir Antiphus of Elide — *Elis*
Came with fifteen ships beside,
And came to Greece, *je vous dy,* — *I tell you (French)*
To passen with that company.
Sir Ulysses, a bold baron,
Swore that Troy should fall a-down,
And brought his host without ween, — *doubt*
And good ships with him fifteen.
Sir Tlepolemus of Rhodes;
He brought ships many and good,
And came to Greece as I thou say,
Where the greater navy lay.
Sir Antiphus of Calydoun, — *Calydna*
Thirty ships he brought all bound,
With all the power of that end,
And ready was to Troy to wend.
Sir Eumelus of Pherae;
Ten vessels he brought him by;
The ships were all good and sure,
Victualled with good armour.
Idomeneus the Lord of Crete;
To wend forth he naught would let. — *delay*
Four score ships he did bring,
Full well victualled in all things.

Sir Eurypylus came also
With fifteen ships and no more,
And a host stout and good
To pass over the salty flood.
Sir Ajax of Locry *Locris*
Came with greater chivalry,
And was ready, swain and knight,
And forty ships, well a-dight.
Nauplius' son, Sir Palamide *Palamedes*
With thirty ships, stout and wide,
And a host stout and good
To passen o'er the salty flood.
Protesilaus, forsooth to tell,
To wend to Troy would he not dwell;
A great host he brought and more,
And forty ships with sail and oar.[28]
Thus did they all together drive
With twelve-hundred ships, fifty and five.[*]
Hearken now unto my spell,
And more of this I will you tell.[29]

How the Greeks sought the answer of the God Apollo, and how King Menelaus appointed his brother Agamemnon Leader of the Host

THEN spake Menelaus, of Greece the King,
To his barons on an evening:
"We must to Apollo sacrifice make
That he may help and for us wake,
The better I hope that we shall do."

[*] Harl. 525: "With twelve-hundred ships, twenty and five"

And all his barons grant thereto.
He took a rich cup for the nonce,
Full of gold and precious stones,
And took his cup with silver and gold
And called a baron that was bold.
"Take," he said, "this rich treasure,
And offer it to Apollo, our saviour,
And learn of him without fail
How we shall speed in our battle."
Dares took the treasure that was fine[30]
And to the Temple of Apolline
It offered as the manner now,
And fell down on his knees also.
"Lord Apollo, I beseech thee,
That thou wilt deign to answer me:
If we shall to battle wend,
How shall we speed at the last end?"
The mammet answered Dares fine:
"Go and war by leave of mine,
And look that ye ne'er stint naught,
'Til Troy be unto ground a-brought!
And ere this ten year be gone,
Ye shall o'ercome them, every one."
Sir Dares heard that tiding
And came to Menelaus the King,
And he told the king his lord
The mammet's answer, every word.
The king then was glad enough,
And for these tidings fast he laughed.
The king called Agamemnon his brother
—He trusted him more than any other—
And constable of his host him makes,
And all his power to him he takes.

The king commanded each a man
To be attendant to Agamemnon:
"For he shall, with much honour,
Be all of your governor."[31]
The king graithèd him to go
And his host, every one.
Now Agamemnon with his chivalry
Sailed o'er the sea full hastily,
With three hundred ships, fifty and five*
That was a fair company to rive.

Of the Embassy of the Greeks and the Third Battle

TO TROY in haste they came to land,
And there they made their ships to stand.[32]
They went on land, every one,
And sent to the King of Troy anon,
And bade that he should him send
Helen the Queen, courteous and hende.
And if they that would do,
With peace again would they go;
If they would not, no other there is:
They would him slay, and all of his.
The King of Troy, Sir Priamus,
Suffered them, and said thus:
"Ye of Greece my father slew,
And my sister hence ye drew;
Therefore I will hold your queen,
Dame Helen, the bright and sheen,

* Harl. 525: "Over the sea they flew away / With twelve hundred ships and five and twenty"

And much maugre come you to,
Lest ye all your worst will do.
I have here, do you understand,
All the power of my land
For to defend, up and down,
Troy that is my richer town."
    The messengers spoke no more now,
But away they did go,
And have told the king, their lord,
Priam's answer, every word.
The folk anon began to ride
And assailed Troy on every side;
They cried and blew, and shot a-fast.
With all manner of engine they did cast;
They had great engines for the nonce,
And cast wondrous mighty stones.
Each turret of the town they did assail,
Twelve months with great battle.

A hundred gins there were upset,
Of mangonels and trebuchet;
The least of them, the sooth to say,
Might cast a large mile of the way.
All about Troy the true,
Night and day they stones in threw.
At every tide their vessels all
Gave assault onto the wall;
Drawn up their boats to the mid-mast,
And shot with darts and arbalest.
And sharp quarrels have also flown
As thick as any hailstone.
So strong assault as there began

Saw ever yet no earthly man
Since that Jesus Christ was born—
Neither after nor before.
They laid on with axes of steel,
And fought together hardy and well.

And they of Troy that were within
Defended with all manner gin.
Each tower was full about the wall
With bow, arbalest, and springald. *catapult*
With good bows and arbalest,
And good slings with stones to cast,
They without the wall did break,
And they within them did a-wreak. *take revenge*
On both parties the folk went down,
But they had the worst without the town.
That first year, with great fight,
Many thousand was to death dight.
So my lords, without fail,
Thus ended the Third Battle.

Of the Fourth Battle, and the prowess of Hector and Alexander

OF ALL *that year for no need,*
They might ne'er against Troy speed.

Anon thereafter Priamus,
The King of Troy, he hath done thus:
He callèd forth beforen him
Two of his sons, stout and grim:
Hector his son that eldest is,
The other Alexander Paris.

"Take your host into the field,
The folk of Greece battle to yield.
Show that ye are doughty knights,
And maintain your father's rights."

And they answered him smartly:
"Father," they said, "we are ready."

Hector and Paris that were stout
Brought their host into the field out,
And were armed well and secure,
And there began a strong bicker.
Sir Hector that stout baron,
Many great lord he felled a-down;
There was no helm, shield nor targe
That might withstand his strokes so large.

And Alexander began to hew;
He felled a hundred in a row.

When Alexander 'gan to smite,
He spared neither much so light;
Many earls and barons of Greece
With their hands they hewed to pieces.

Great slaughter was made on every side
Of horse, of men, in fields wide.
All the valleys ran with blood;
There died many a freely fode. *noble youth*

Thus they fought with sword and spear
Many months of the year.*

* Harl. 525: "Nine months of the year"

In Troy they rested every night,
And on the morrow again to fight.
The folk of Greece upon their side
Took a truce for to abide
'Til dead bodies were buried in ground,
And heal them that had a wound;
The King of Troy granted their boon
Until the year were all done.
So my lords, without fail,
Thus ended the Fourth Battle.

Of the Fifth Battle, and how Protesilaus and Patroclus were slain by Hector

THE fourth year Hector the warrior
Brought his host with great honour
Out of Troy into the field,
Himself on steed with spear and shield.
The folk of Greece he destroys,
And they against him harder drives.
A duke of Greece, Protesilaus,
Came pricking upon his horse.

Against Hector a stroke he wound;
The shaft it shivered in his hand.
They brought out swords, sharply ground;
Each gave other grimly wound.
They struck fast them between
With swords that were sharp and keen,
That fire out of the helms hath sprang.
Between them was battle strong
That no man could the truth say

Which of them might the better be.
Sir Hector then a struck a wound
—I would you all to understand,
Was ne'er such smiting ere that day,
Certainly, as I you say— — *as I tell you*
The flesh quit he pared a-down,
Both through hauberk and aketon. — *coat of mail and the jacket worn beneath*
And, as God gave him grace,
It made the sword somedeal glance
That halfendeal the broad shield — *half of*
Freely flew into the field.
But Sir Hector anon him hit,
That head from body off he smit. — *smote*

Sir Hector smote him with his spear
That from his saddle he did bear.[33]
Then came Sir Patroclus, a lord,
And other warriors, many and good,
All they laid Sir Hector on
And he defended as a man.[*]

He laid about him with good speed;
942 *Many a side he made to bleed.*

Patroclus' body he smote a-two;
A hundred knights he slew also.[34]
Thus lasted that sorry play
Forty days, day by day.
Menestheus, a noble baron,
Would joust with Hector, the champion,

[*] Harl. 525: "But he defended as a lion"

And with his spear rode him nigh,
And smote Sir Hector through the thigh.
When Hector saw his blood run down
He waxed eager as any lion;
Hector did slay with sword's dint
Sixty men ere then he stint.*
And his brother Alexander Paris,
He felled down many knight of prize.

How Alexander wounded Sir Menelaus with an arrow, and how the Greeks asked for a truce of six months to bury their dead

THE King of Greece saw Paris his foe;
To him he cried and said so:
"Traitor, deliver my queen so bright,
That thou hold'st with much un-right,
Or thou shalt say, ere we're gone,
Full evil bale thou her won!" *torment; suffering*
And either would to other win,
But the host did start between.
From a man a bow Paris took
And drew an arrow to the hook,
And smote the king through the side
For all his armour a wound wide.
A leech anon the arrow drew out
And healed the king, well enough.[35]
No man might number, without lies,
The folk that on both sides slain was.

* Harl. 525: "A thousand men ere ever he stint"

The way was full of men's blood
Where the men rode and yode. *went*
There was slain so many folk
That in blood ran every polke; *puddle; pool*
Men might not finden a bare stead
But upon dead men to tread.

When the folk began to fail
Anon departs that strong battle;
And they of Troy went into town,
And they of Greece to pavilion,
And made a peace on either side
Half a year to abide.
The dead bodies they laid in ground,
And healed them that had a wound.
All the wounded healed fast,
And the dead in earth were cast.
So my lords, without fail,
Thus ended the Fifth Battle.

How Palamedes told the Greeks of the mighty Achilles

WHEN the time of truce was come to end
They made them ready to battle to wend,
And dight them fast on either side
With all that might go or ride.
The King of Greece, Sir Menelae,
He called before him on a day
Agamemnon his brother, iwis,
That constable o'er his host was,
To earls and to many baron,
And other lords of great renown,

And said, "My lords, see ye not
How our folk are to ground brought?
Lest ye work wise-like, or better you ta'en, *take better care*
Hector will slay us, every man.
Therefore now, I pray thou,
Everyone for his own prow, *benefit*
That ye slay Hector if ye may;
Then have we mastery for e'er and aye."
Then answered a clerk, and said right
(Master Palamedes I wot he hight),
"Sire King," he said, "hearken to me,
And good counsel I shall give ye:
No man alive in all this world
May slay Hector with dint of sword
But a child that was wight and hardier,
And was born in the land of Phthia.
And if thou that child have might,
He shall slay Hector, that doughty knight.

"For a man, the god of Libye, *Libya*
He showed me full utterly
In a planet, verrament, *verily*
He shall him slay with doleful dint.

"Achilles is the child's name;[36]
His mother a witch can mighty shame.
If ye will a moment dwell,
Of that child I will you tell;
How he was gotten hearken now,
For all men witten not how.
Half-man, half-horse his father was,
And he was called Sir Peleus.[37]
His mother a goddess of the sea;

Half-fish and half-woman was she.
And her name was Dame Thetis;
Of her was gotten Achilles.
    "When he was born, without fail,
That he should be strong in battle
His mother bathed him, verrament,
In water of enchantèment
That so hard became his skin
As baleen to hewen in—
All but the soles of his feet
Where his mother's hands were set."
    (And since he was slain there,
As ye hereafter shall now hear).
    "When Achilles was seven years old
He was wise and of speech bold.
And thus was his father wont
For to gear his young son
To wade in the deep sea far in,
And make him stand up to the chin
To fight against the waves great—
And if he fell he would him beat.
And yet he made the child more do,
To take the lion's whelps her from;
And for he was so hard of skin
They might no damage do to him.
    Upon a day the Dame Thetis
To the firmament looked, without lies,
And there she saw, without fail,
Her son should be slain in battle.
Therefore his mother was full woe,
And said, 'Certain, it shall not be so!'
And sent him to the land of Parchy[38] *Sparta*
In maid's attire, cleverly,

And said Achilles was it naught,
But his sister they had brought.
Sir Lycomedes was the king;
He had a daughter that was young.
Deidamia was her name;
Much she knew of glee and game.

"She was a lovely creáture,
Gentle and sweet, of fair porture. deportment
Lovely were her eyen too;
Gracious vice she had also.

"So long Achilles was in bower
With the maidens of honour,
The king's daughter in child was."

How the Knights of Greece feasted at the court of the King Lycomedes, and how Sir Achilles was knighted by the same king

HEARETH now a wondrous case:
Knights of Greece came hastily
Into the land of Parchy

That comen from Sir Menelae.
1058 *And in that land comen were they*

To see Achilles that was so wight;
In the king's court they found him right.
And soon they came to that city;
There was the king and his company.
That day the knights, without lying,
Ate with Lycomedes the King.

They were servèd richèly,
With meats and drinks noblèy;
With swans and cranes and bitterns,
Plover, partridge, and wild boars,
With curlews and cormorant,
With mallards wild and pheasant.
And when the cloth was drawn away,
Then beginneth now to play
A hundred minstrels in a row,
Diverse melody to show
Of trumpets, tabors, and nakers, — *types of drum*
Pipers, psalterers, and cymbalers. — *players of a psaltery, a stringed instrument*

And when they all eaten had,
The king's daughter the dancing led.

Her name was Deidamides, — *Deidamia*
And led in her hand Achilles.

Achilles was great and long withal;
The king's daughter was gentle and small.
Achilles had a stout visage,
And was full gay, and savage.

All the knights that there was
Beheld e'ermore on Achilles;
How he was so stout and grim,
And inwardly behelden him
And said it was never woman,
So large of shape, body, and bone.

The knights said, every one,
That it was never a woman,
And took their counsel there anon
Ere they would hence go on,
To give the maidens brooch and ring
And to Achilles give nothing
But a hauberk and a spear,
To Achilles would they bear.

And when they came unto the place
They would lay it on the grass,
And said, "If he be Achilles,
He will it have, without lies."

When Achilles saw that thing
He, forsaking brooch and ring,
To kind armour he would take,
And brooch and ring he would forsake.
And on the morrow, without lying,
Also they ate with the king;
And when they had eaten and board was ta'en,
The maidens danced, every one.
The knights gave them brooch and ring,
But Achilles gave they no such thing;
They laid before him shield and spear,
And all manner armour knight should wear.
Achilles stood and beheld right
The armour that was fair and bright,
And on him soon he did it cast,
And in that attire went in haste.
And when he was armed in iron and steel,
This him likèd wondrous well.[39]
So spake Achilles hastily:

"Sir King, bright armour wear will I!
In maiden's dance I will not go,
But armour bright will I me to.
Therefore Sire King, now pray I thee,
Dub me knight with charity,
And give me armour, shield and spear,
And steed good my body to bear!

"I am Achilles, so mote I then,
Stronger than any of thy men,
And may God give me mischance
If I go more unto your dance!
To the Battle of Troy I will right
To prove my main and my might:
Give me horse and arms also,
And make me knight and let me go!"

Anon the king him dubbed as knight;
In rich attire then he was dight,
And gave him armour good and sure
With of lion a goodly fur,
And good steeds he gave him to
And bade him swift to Troy to go,
The King of Greece to succour
Both in battle and in stour. *Conflict*

How Achilles was welcomed by the Greeks

HE WENT to Troy fast as he may
To help the king, Sir Menelae.
When Achilles was come to Troy
The Grecians made them mickle joy.

Sir Menelaus, of Greece the King,
Welcomed Achilles in all things,
And said, "Achilles, I tell thee
Of thine help great need have we.
For Sir Priam, of Troy the King,
Hath a son—a fair youngling—
And is a man of mickle might:
A bolder man came ne'er in fight.
There is no man upon our side
That dare his strokes in battle abide.

"Therefore Achilles, I pray thee
With him to fight when thou him see;
For were he to ground to fall
We should be masters of them all."

Achilles answered him thereto:
"All that I may I will do.
I swear, Sire, by god Mahoun, *Mohammed or the devil*
However strong a champion,
The first time I may to Hector win
He shall me slay, or I will him."
Achilles' mother was a witch, iwis;
She taught her son a fair quaintness:
How he should keep him whole and sound,
And come from battle without wound.
Achilles did then primèly,
As his mother taught him cleverly
With witchcraft and nigromancy there 'til *black magic*
His mother him bathed in the water of Hell.
He was hanged by the feet and thrice dipped down,
Body and blood, head and crown—
All but the soles of his feet

Where his mother's hands did sit.
And his head was black as Mahoun
From the feet unto the crown,
And all his body was hard as flint
That was good against dint.
When Achilles was thus dight
He armed him well in armour bright,
And to the field anon he rides,
And with the king in battle abides.

Of the dream of Andromache, and how King Priam forbade his son Hector from riding into battle that day

SIR Priamus of Troy the King
With his host was ready in all things,
And Hector and Sir Paris
That were knights of great prize.
Then came forth Sir Hector's wife
That loved her lord as her life:
She cried and wept tenderly
And said, "Lord King, I cry mercy!
Tonight, at about midnight
In my dream me thought aright
If Hector my lord to battle goes
He will be slain among his foes.
And therefore, Lord, I you pray:
Make him dwell at home today!"
    Then answered Priamus the King:
"Hector, for chance of thy wife's dreaming,
Dwell at home with thy lady hende—
We be enough to battle to wend."

Of the Sixth Battle, and the prowess of Achilles

HECTOR then at home abides,
And his father with his host forth rides,
And each the other did assail—
There began a strong battle.
Many thousand were slain, sans fail.[40] *without fail*
Thus they fought, the knights stout,
Forty days, out and out.
Of barons, knights, and other vitail, *soldiers(?)*
Five hundred thousand dead, sans fail.

There might men see, without lying,
Good knights by their stirrups hung;
Many a helm there was off-weaved,
And many bascinet there was cleaved. *a medieval helmet*
Many a spear and many a shield
Flew about into the field.
There were many wounds wide,
And also many a bloody side,
And many losing their heart's blood,
And many on the balls in the hood; *on the heads in their*
Many brained into the head, *helmets or hoods*
And many good steed its life bereaved.
Many a knight lost both his arms,
And many a steed trailed its tharms. *intestines; entrails*
Many a doughty man in the field
Lay there slain under shield.

No man might see for no good
In all the field but the blood;
In great rivers the blood did run,

Of horse and bodies of dead men.
And e'er Achilles sought up and down
After Hector, the champion.
But Achilles might not meet with him,
For he was not in the field that time.

That time Achilles hath undertaken
That Hector is not to battle comen,
He laid about him in length and breadth,
1204 *And cried, "Traitors, ye be dead!"*

When Achilles might meet with him naught,
He met an earl that dear it bought;
Achilles the earl hard strikes,
And his body a-two soon smites.
Another he hit upon the shield
That head and helm flew in the field.
The third knight he sparèd naught:
Horse and man to death he brought.
Down to the saddle he clove the fourth;
All that he smote went to the earth.
As a wode lion fared he *mad; enraged*
That had fasted for days three.
The King of Troy saw Achilles ride,
And fled with his host and durst not 'bide.
Achilles hunted the host all
Right to Troy—the castle wall.
Achilles won the mastery;
The King of Greece was glad forthy. *therefore*
So my lords, without fail,
Thus ended the Sixth Battle.

Of the Seventh Battle, and the meeting of Hector and Achilles

IT WAS *upon the Pentecost,*
Such time as the Holy Ghost
Alighted down in form of fire,
Among his Apostles with glad cheer.

Hector in a tower stands and sees
How Priamus his father flees.
"Alas," said Hector, "that I was born!
My father's honour today is lorn. *lost*
I ne'er shall while I may go or ride
See my father such a hap betide.
And namely for a woman's dream—
Of feeble comfort, indeed I am!"

He armed himself in steel weed *steel clothing (armour)*
1228 *And leapt upon a noble steed.*

Hector armed him hastily;
Forsooth, it turned to great folly.
When that Hector was ready bound
He went him forth out of the town,
And prickèd forth with might and main,
And all the host he drove again.
His own body ere he stint
Slew thirty knights with his dint.

Hector did slay with doleful dint
A thousand men ere ever he stint;
Was never knight since God was born
—Neither since, and nor before—

That bore him better, without delay,
Than did Hector on that day.
But he was slain with doleful cheer,
As ye may hereafter hear.

Soon Achilles with Hector met;
There were strokes hard a-set.

For never in this world were seen
Two stronger knights, as I ween.

Hector hard on Achilles strikes
With his sword that well bites.
He smote Achilles with great ire
That from his helm there sprang a fire;
And Achilles, with might and main,
Smote Sir Hector hard again[41]
That a quarter of his shield
Flew away into the field.
And Hector hard on Achilles strikes,
With his sword that well bites;
The sword was sharp and well keen,
That on Achilles' head t'was seen
The circle of gold down he felled,
That it flew into the field.

Hector sees he's with his maker met;
Strokes on Achilles sore he set
That his shield to pieces flayed,
And a side of his gambeson away; *a padded jacket*
Hauberk and aketon also,
And his thigh well-nigh in two.[42]

In the saddle the sword withstood;
Achilles is grievèd well-nigh wode.

Now Achilles began to smite,
And sparèd Hector but a lite; *little*
He smote Hector upon his shield
That a quarter flew into the field.

And when his shield was smashed to naught
Soon he was another brought.
A new battle, without lies,
Began 'tween Hector and Achilles;
Might no man know, for swords bright,
Which of them was the better knight.

Between them the battle was strong,
And hard strokes they gave among.
With swords they hewed upon helms clear;
They would not stand on no manner.
Hector was wroth, man enough;
His good sword forth he draweth,
And smote Achilles on the crown
That his helm to pieces fell a-down.
The sword upon the shoulder glad, *glided*
And sheared the hauberk a hand broad.
Aketon, kirtle it sheared a-two;
Further than kirtle it might not go.
The skin ne'er might it pierce naught
With no weapon that e'er was wrought.
Achilles was bathed in the water of Hell:
Therefore no man might him quell.
His skin was hard as any flint

That was good against dint.
When Achilles was thus smitten,
He was wroth—well may ye witten.
To avenge him he had good will,
And smote Hector full hard 'til
Upon his shoulder, God it wot,
That the sword the shoulder bit
Half a foot and somedeal more;
The blood made red what white was 'fore.
When Hector saw his blood run down
We waxed as wode as any lion,
And smote Achilles in that stound
That he fell unto the ground.
But Achilles fared ne'er the worse.
Now Hector anon turned his horse;
Toward Troy he began to ride,
And would no longer there abide.
Hector saw that with no ill
Achilles might he ne'er come 'til;
Hector flew upon his steed,
And Achilles followed with good speed.

How Hector, taken at a disadvantage, was slain by Achilles

IN THE *morn Priam the King*
Was ready in all manner thing;
And all that e'er doth Hector meet,
Soon began their lives to let.
Then came soon a champion
—A lord of Greece of great renown—
That was called Sir Polypoetes:

He was a man of much prize.
He was attired in good armour
That shone as gold and azure.
The helm was rich, for the nonce,
Set about with precious stones;
With rubies and sapphires oriental,
With chalcedonies great and small.
Fast he 'gan Hector to assail,
And he might with strong battle.
Sir Hector anon him hit;
Both helm and head off he smit.
Sir Hector saw that rich attire,
And thereto had great desire.

As Hector pricked upon his way
He saw a helm where it lay[43]
That was rich, for the nonce,
All beset with precious stones,
And loath he would the helm forgo;
Therefore he lost worth the two.
He lost his life for that helm's sake;
For Hector in Troy great sorrow they make.
Hector to the helm rode right;
Therethrough died that doughty knight.
He leaned over his steed's mane,
The rich helm up to ta'en;
Achilles came riding, verrament,
And smote him at the fundament.
To the heart he smote him right;
Thus ended that doughty knight.

And then died the doughtiest man
That e'er lived since the world began.
The King of Troy this then sees;
With woe and sorrow to town he flees.

The light of day began to fail;
Then departed that great battle.

They of Troy have gone to town,
And they of Greece to pavilion.

Upon the morrow for either's sake
On both halves a truce they take;
A year full by both their rede
While they buried all the dead.
Then either king now full wide
Sent after folk on each side, *sought reinforcements*
And also purveyed more victuals.
Thus can end the Seventh Battle.

Of the sorrowful lamentation of King Priamus for the death of his son Hector

KING Priamus and all his
Made great sorrow—no wonder 'tis—
For Hector that doughty champion.
They went with great processìon
And fetched Hector out of the field;
Alas, turned up was his shield.
He was buried with great honour
Before the gates of the tower;

All the folk of that city
For him made sorrow and pity.

And Sir Priam, as I you say, — *as I tell you*
Wept and sorrowed night and day;
For Hector, the good warrior,
He wrung his hands and drew his hair.
"Alas," he said, "what me is woe!
Why will my heart not break in two?"
With that he fell unto the ground
And swoonèd in that very stound;
It was great dole, so God me glade, — *gladden*
To see the lamenting that he made.

How Achilles became enamored of Dame Polyxena, the daughter of King Priam

ACHILLES 'bout the city rides;
Seldom in pavilion he abides.
Upon a time he comes and sees
Where that Hector buried is,
And nearby stood a maiden sheen:
The king's daughter, Dame Polyxene

Come unto that very place
Where her brother slain was.
A little beside the grave she stood;
She wept and wrung her hands in blood.

She wept and sorrowed and many another,
And bemoaned Hector her brother.

"Alas, alas," then said she,
"That I now this day should see
So doughty a body in that stound, — *in death*
That so low is laid in the ground!"
Such dole she made for him now
That nigh her heart did break in two.
Her lovely hair shined as silk;
Her lovesome face, white as milk.
She all to-drew her rich gear;
She rent her face and tore her hair,
And often called herself caitiff, — *a wretch*
And said, "Too long I last in life!"

Achilles stood and beheld right
The maiden that was fair and bright;
How she was dight in silver and gold,
And thought the fairest maid on mold, — *on earth*
And 'gan to love the maiden so
That nigh his heart would burst in two.
He would have spoken with her there,
But for her friends he did spare.

How Achilles made an offer of peace to King Priam in exchange for the hand of Dame Polyxena, and of the king and queen's answer

TO HIS pavilion rode him right,
And unto him he called a knight:
"Go to Troy and tell King Priamus
That I thee send to say thus:
That for a woman this war was waked,

And for a woman peace shall be maked.
For Dame Helen, the Queen of Greece,
Many men have been hewn to pieces;
To me his daughter if he will swore,
There shall be peace for ever more.
If he and his goodly queen
Will give their daughter Polyxene,
Her to be mine own countess,
All the harms I will redress.
For good were peace on either side,
Lest more harm will betide."
The knight went to Priam the King
And told him this new tiding.
Priamus said, "Nay," truly,
He would not her give to his enemy.
"That day shall me ne'er betide,
The while I may go and ride!"

Sir Priamus answered in hie
That he that was his enemy
Should ne'er his daughter have to wife;
For no man that beareth life
—And namely that had slain his son!—
First he should be hanged and drawn.
Troilus and Alexander Paris,
The kings sons, both wit and wise,
Rebukèd so this messenger
That he repented coming there.

Then spoke the queen, his own wife:
"Sir, good is," she said, "to stint strife.
Go to thy lord Achilles

So that he make perpetual peace;
So that never warring be,
We shall him give our daughter free."
    The knight took leave with good accord
And came and told his lord each word:
"If ye will make peace without end,
Ye shall have their daughter hende."

Of the answer of Menelaus the King

ACHILLES was glad of that tiding,
And went to Menelaus the King
And said to the king, without lies,
He was about to make a peace.

"And better in peace and rest to wend
Than live in war without end."

    The King of Greece, Sir Menelae
Answered Achilles and said, "Nay!
To peace will I never counsel;
They be o'ercome in plain battle.
For now Hector is to death fall,
I'll not give a sore for them all." *I don't care*

He said to him these words right:
"Though thy love be on a lady light,
Amends have I never none
Of the wrong they have me done;
Of robbery and ravishing my queen
—Helen that is so bright and sheen—

And 'til this time withhold her there;
Lest I be wreaken it ruth me sore. — *lest I be avenged*
And therefore," he said now, — *I will regret it*
"Consent shall I never to
Until I wit, without fail,
Who shall win the battle."

Achilles in wrath went away,
And lived in longing all that day.

The love of Polyxene him takes,
That great sorrow for her he makes.
He droops and dares, night and day; — *lies motionless*
Often bemoans that lovesome maid,
Her fair semblance and lovely cheer;
Her rode red as blossom on briar. — *complexion*
Her lovely face, her lips sweet.
His sorrow is much, and unmeet, — *improper*
And thus he sigheth day and night,
And oft bemoaneth that sweet wight. — *creature; person*

Of the wrath of Achilles, and the prowess of Sir Troilus

WHEN time of truce had come to end
They made them ready, battle to wend.
[The King of Greece with his host rides;][44]
Achilles at home in wrath abides,[45]
And the King of Troy comen is,
And his son Alexander Paris,
And his other son, a young knight
—Sir Troilus was his name a-right—

And earls and barons with much pride,
And began the battle in that tide. time

One of the greatest, I understand,
That e'er befell in any land;
And whoso of the battle will
Now aft may hear, if ye be still.

All that summer the battle did last;
Many a knight other down cast.
Alexander Paris and his brother
Slew the lords, one and other.

There men might soon see
Legs a-cut by the knee,
And many a man was bored through,
That lay weltering in many furrow.
Many a helm there was to-riven,
And many a shield all to-cloven;
Many a hauberk there was to-hewn,
And many a face with blood be-rained.
Many was the shirt stained with blood;
There died many a freely fode.
And ere the battle were overcome,
There died many a mother's son.

Troilus wounded the Greek king now,
And Agamemnon his brother too,
And would have brought them to dead,
But they flew away for dread.
The King of Greece fled with his barons;
The Trojans robbed their pavilions

Of treasure, horse, and their attire,
And many ships they set on fire.[46]

How the King of Greece persuaded Achilles to enter the battle

NOW *shall ye hear of Achilles;*
When of bed arisen was,
Toward the battle he came riding
And met with Menelaus the King.

The King of Greece came to Achilles
And set him down upon his knees
And said, "Sir Achilles, I cry mercy,
That thou us help and that in hie!
In the battle was a knight beardless,
Thrice stalwart as Hector e'er was.

"Sorely wounded hath he me,
And my brother, as thou may see.
Also stern he is in fight,
As a lion outrages on height.

"There is no man that may stand
The strokes he gave them with his hand;
Therefore help us at this need,
Or else certain we are but dead!

"Through him we have lost this fight—
Cowards we be called full right."
Achilles answered to the king:
"Sire, I wonder of thy talking

That he so strong a man is,
And is naught but a child, iwis.
There is no man so strong of kind
But that he may his maker find.
And yet today men shall see
The which of us shall master be!"
Achilles armeth him aright
In armour sheen as the sun bright,
And upon him a noble corselet.
The helm upon the head is set—
Better wore it yet no man.
It was the king's, Sir Laomedon;
In Troy it won Sir Hercules,
When he won the Golden Fleece.
The helm was dight richèly
With pipes of gold and rich pery, precious stones
With carbuncles shining bright,
And peridots of much might; an olive-green gem
With rubies and sapphires oriental,
And all was set with rich enamel.
A richer helm was never under sun
Since the world was begun.
His shield about his neck he cast,
And leaped to horse all in haste.
He smote his steed with spurs of gold;
Many a man did him behold.

Of the Eighth Battle, and the death of young Troilus

ACHILLES came pricking on his steed;
Of Troilus he taketh good heed.

And of Troilus he had a sight,
And ascried him anon right:
"Abide, thou young bachelor,
For thou more shall find here;
Ere that thou this battle win,
Another play thou must begin!
I am Achilles that to thee speak;
Our King of Greece I will awreak.
Turn thee hither, and fight with me!"
"With good cheer," said Troilus, "so mote I thee!"

Such a stroke he hath him wrought
That his shield went to naught;
And Troilus sore aggrievèd was,
And smote a dint to Achilles
That his shield in pieces flew to ground.
Again Achilles in that stound
Smote a stroke onto his shield
That helm and head flew in the field.
Another he smote in that stound,
And smote him dead unto the ground.[47]
The third, the fourth, that he hits,
All that he smites he all to-slits.

Even atwo his body he dealed;
Found he no man that him healed.
Another baron he met with,
That horse and man to earth he slayeth.

The king fled and durst not abide
When he saw Achilles so ride,
And Achilles followed the host all
Right unto the city wall.
Now took they a truce for half a year
And healed them that wounded were,
And buried the dead bodies, good speed,
And purveyed all they had of need.
So my lords, without fail,
Thus ended the Eighth Battle.

How Hecuba the Queen purposed to slay Achilles by treason

THE King of Troy was in great dread,
For his folk were brought to dead.
He made firm his ditches up and down
And set good watch over the town,
And commanded his bailiffs far and wide
To fetch more folk on every side.
The Queen of Troy, Sir Priam's wife,
In great sorrow led her life;
For Troy and her sons she sickened sore,
And said thus for evermore:
"Achilles traitor, e'er be thou woe
That Troilus slain and Hector both.
My whole heart will burst in five
Lest I be wreaken, and that blive! *avenged*
Alexander, son, come now to me;
My dear son, I pray to thee,
On my blessing do by my rede
And awreak thy brethren that be dead."
Alexander answered, "Mother, how

Should I awreak my brethren now?
For in this world was ne'er man found
That may Achilles bring to ground.

"For as hard is his skin and bone
As is baleen to hew upon.

"How should I then bring him down?"
"Yes son," she said, "with treason.

"I tell thee, son, utterly,
There is a place of his body
In the soles of his feet
Where his mother's hands were set,
When she bathed him, verrament,
With water of enchantèment.
Might'st thou with some wile come thereto,
Son Paris, thou shouldst him there slew.

"He hath desired many a day
To wed my daughter that fair maid;
Therefore I shall to him send
That he shall to the temple wend,
And wed my daughter with much honour,
Polyxena, white as flour.
And therefore to the temple go
With a hundred men of arms or more,
And when he is hither come,
Quick or dead that he be nome."
And Paris chose him up and down
Men of arms of great renown—
A hundred men that could fight,
And hid them in the temple by night.

And held them therein, close and still,
And thought them for to have their will.

The queen sent to Achilles by treason;
The messenger went out of the town,
Greeted him well, and said thus:
"Hither me sent King Priamus,
And said he would no more battle
For his folk begin to fail,
And will soften all with peace
And give ye his daughter, Achilles.
To the temple ye should wend
And wed ye there his daughter hende,
And half his kingdom have with her.
Therefore haste you swiftly, Sire,
And whom thou wilt with you take,
And go to the temple, sureness to make."

Achilles saw that he was free;
He gave him gifts of great plenty.
He wist nothing of his treason,
Nor of their false conspiration.

How Achilles entered the temple to wed Dame Polyxena, and instead was slain there

ACHILLES dight him rich and gay
—For he lovèd much that maid—
And clad him in a fair shroud,
For to wed her he was proud.
He lapped him in a cape of sendal, *silk*

And took his sword and did well.
Of all his folk told he none
Whither that he would be gone,
But a young knight with him he led.[48]
Indeed he was full hard bestood, *ready to serve*
And proudly to the temple came
—Of no treason wist he then—
And came hastily therein;
The door they stuck upon him.

Therewhile a man, well I wot,
Smote him in the soles of his feet,
And gave him a wound unride; *savage; cruel*
The knights start up on every side.

They cried, "Traitor! Yield ye anon!"
And he answered now full soon:
"I was never traitor, truly,
And that soon I will prove to ye!"
About his arm his mantle laps,
And drew his sword; to them he swaps,
And wounded them and did them harm,
And smote off heads and also arms.
His fellow was slain anon right,
But he defended as a knight.
They ne'er might him do no dere, *hurt; harm*
Neither with sword nor with spear.
He stood full hard against their dint;
His skin was hard as any flint.
In many steads he gave them wound:
Sixty of them he brought to ground
With sword, and they assailed him fast;
Achilles defended while his life did last.

So hard he smote unto them now
That his sword did burst a-two.

Now he was in a feeble case:
"Alas!" he said, helpless. "Alas!"
With his fist he laid on fast,
That their necks fast he burst.

Achilles stirred him, for need him teaches;
With the shoulders to one he reaches,
Slung them about and let them go
That they to-burst against the stone.
Another he flung against a wall,
And there he died among them all.
The third he took in his armour stout
And cast him at a window out.
As a hungry lion fared he
That had fasted for days three.
So with strokes he did them drive;
Of a hundred twenty left alive.
All the blood of that man
In sweat out of his body ran;
Now waxed him feeble, and t'was no ferly— *no wonder*
His heart's blood was all dreary
That all perceivèd anon right,
And spake to Achilles, that good knight:
"Traitor, thou shalt to death go!"
With his sword he smote Achilles so.

Alexander spoke him to:
"Now thou shalt thy life forgo!
Thou slew Hector, the good warrior,
And Troilus, brother, life and dear!"

And since they twenty all at once
So fain they were to break his bones,
They put Achilles down to ground
And 'neath his feet they gave him wound
With the sword and with long knife;
Thus they reaved him of his life.
Thus was he slain with treason,
And by the legs drawn out of town.
The King of Troy commanded on high
—Without horn or outcry—
Into the field men should him bear,
That wild beasts might him tear.

That men should bend an engine
And thereupon they should lay him
And cast him to the King of Greece,
That hounds might gnaw him into pieces.

And he swore great oaths then:
"He was a devil, and no man!"
And thus ended Achilles there:
In all the world he had no peer.[49]

How Menelaus the King would have revenge for the murder of Achilles, and of the prowess of Alexander

SIR Menelaus of Greece the King
Heard tell of that sorry tiding;
How Achilles his good baron
Was cruelly slain with foul treason.
He made sorrow and was full woe,

And all his barons called him to
And said, "To arms, my lordings!
Each man be graithèd in all things.
For Achilles avenged be shall,
Or we should lose our lives all!"
    He took his host and forth he hied,
And came to Troy and them destroyed.
And Priamus of Troy also,
Alexander Paris and others more,
They them graithed on either side
With all that might go or ride,
And went against their enemies
And laiden on them hard, iwis,
With sword and spear and with knife;
Thirty thousand there lost their life.
And thus they fought, without fail,
Twenty days with strong battle.
Alexander was in the vanguard;
There was no man that he spared.
Earl, baron, knight nor swain,
No man might him stand against.
Many of Greece he brought to ground
And gave him death with spear's wound.

He laid on as he were wode;
That day was spilled so much blood
That no man might ever tell
The folk that on both sides fell.
There was many a bloody side,
And many a wound, deep and wide;
Many was bored through the lung,
And many through with spears strong.

Many steed there broke its back,
And many lost the head in his iron hat.
Such hurtling was on each side,
Horse and man lay dead in fields wide;
It seemed of helms and swords bright
As though it had from Heaven alight.
This battle lasted, without miss,
—As books of grammar bear witness—
A full twelve days, day by day;
Thus they fought with doleful play.
When twelve days to the end was brought,
Then was the most sorrow wrought
That e'er befell in any land,
As far as I do understand,
For then ended Sir Alexander.[50]

How Sir Ajax slew Alexander with a spear, and in so doing received a mortal wound

AJAX of Greece, a noble baron;
He was a man of great renown.
He came pricking with spear and shield
To joust with Paris in the field,
And Paris took a spear also
And against Ajax he rode now,
And made his spear so nigh him glide
That the spear head left in his side.
There was Ajax smote full sore,
But he thought to joust some more;
Sir Ajax rode againward,
And smote Alexander full hard

—Through the shield to the heart right—
And thus died that doughty knight.

Jesus, that ruleth day and night,[51]
As thou died'st for all mankind
To wash them out of their sin,
On their souls have pity,
If that it thy will should be.

Knights of Troy that were there
Took up Paris and home did bear,
And buried him by Hector his brother.
His father sorrowed and many another,
And Dame Helen his queen also;
She wept for him and was full woe,
And said, "Alexander, wellaway! *alas*
Why fetched thou me from Greece away
With strength hither to be thy wife?
Therefore hast thou lost thy life!"
Down she fell aswoon him by,
And knights took her up in hie.[52]

Of the death of Sir Ajax, and how the City of Troy was besieged for six months

LET we now Alexander be,
And of Sir Ajax speak we:
Ajax to his pavilion rides
With the spear's head in his side,
And said he might go and ride
With the spear's head out of his side.

But when it was out of the knight
Sir Ajax died, anon right.[53]
Then spake Menelaus the King,
And called his barons on evening
And said, "Now hath Paris his meed, *reward*
For he away my wife did lead.
Now is his treason well yield: *well repaid*
I am quick and he is under mold.
Therefore full secure am I—
We getten now the mastery.
We be enough stiff and stout;
Go we besiege them all about!
We shall them slay at our own will,
Or they shall for hunger spill."
And when the king had thus said,
They were armed and soon graithèd,
And besieged Troy on each side
That no man might go nor ride
With meat nor drink, far nor near:
Thus was Troy besieged for half a year.
So my lords, without fail,
Thus ended the Tenth Battle.[54]

Of the foul treason of Antenor and Aeneas

So it befell in the beginning of May,
When fowl sing upon each spray
And blossoms break upon each bough,
And over all was mirth enough.
But in Troy was no mirth now:
Sir Priamus the King was woe,
And called his barons to him full soon

And said, "My lords, what shall we do?
Were my son now alive
He would our foemen from us drive.
Or his brother, Alexander Paris;
Little would we doubt of our enemies.
I am now old, witterly,
And ne'er may go to war, forthy,
But ye be enough stalwart and stout:
Take your host in the field without,
The men of Greece to assail,
And slay them down in battle
And show ye are doughty of deed—
Full well I hope that all ye speed."
    Then answered a baron, a faitour— *deceiver; imposter*
Sir Antenor, a foul traitor:
"Lord," he said, "we should out go
And awreak you on your foe."
Now went Antenor full good pace
To another traitor, Aeneas.[55]
"Aeneas," he said, "what to rede?
If we go to battle we are dead.
If we dwell still and defend the town
For hunger we shall fall a-down.
Therefore at night we will wend out
To the King of Greece that is stout,
And bid him grant limb and life
And save us, both child and wife,
And we will Troia to him yield—
Better this than die in field."
Aeneas granted thereto soon,
And plighted truths it should be done.
    Antenor and Aeneas anon them dight,
And out at a postern went by night

And came to Menelaus, of Greece King.
Antenor spake first the beginning
And said, "Lord," thus and thus,
"Ye besiege our king, Sir Priamus,
But certain with no skins gin, *clever disguises/deceits(?)*
Troia thou shalt never win.
For all that thou might do ever,
The city of Troy win ye never.
Will ye grant us two our lives,
And our children and our wives,*
And all our goods for evermore,
If we shall let in you and yours
This same night that cometh next,
When ye be in to do your best?"
The King of Greece answered him now:
"Make me secure ere ye go,
And either of you your truth me plight
To let us come in this same night.
And as I am a true king
I shall you save in all things—
With wife and child and with land,
And thereto I hold up my hand."
The traitors anon plight their truth;
To betray their lord it was a ruth. *pity*
They took their leave those traitors both,
And betrayed their lord—aye worth them woe.
On the morrow they went up and down
And comforted those in the town,
And bade the folk with all their might
Keep well the wards that very night.
They bade the king he should naught spare

* Harl. 525: "Our cattle, children, and our wives"

To make him merry without care,
And said it was by their counsel
That he began that same battle;.
Therefore they told him that they would
Against his foes the city hold.
The king said, "Blessed must ye be,
And all my barons that helped me."
The king said quit them he would *reward*
With rich rents and with gold.[56]

How King Menelaus entrusted the capture of the city to young Pyrrhus

WHEN night was come and gone the day
The King of Greece, Sir Menelae,
Commanded his host to graith them still
And said they should have all their will.
The king callèd before him right
Achilles' son—a noble knight.
He was a doughty man and fair;
Prince of Myrmidons, his father's heir.*
His name was callèd Sir Pyrrhus;[57]
The King of Greece spoke to him thus:
"Wilt thou avenge thy father now?"
"Full fain, Lord, and I wist how."
The king said, "Take half my host
Right privily, without boast,
And go to the city right full soon—
The bridge is down and the gates undone.
Call Antenor and Aeneas,

* Harl. 525: "Prince of Macedon, his father's heir. / He hight Sir Neoptolemus"

Save their lives and let them pass,
And raise thy banner when thou art in—
Thus thou shalt the city win.
And slay cleanly up and down
All that thou findest in the town,
And we shall without it be
To keep that no man away flee."

Of the slaughter of the Trojans

PYRRHUS went right to the gate
And found the traitors ready thereat;
He let them at the gates forth pass,
And slew the others, more and less.
In at the gates they did drive,
And raisèd up his banner swithe;
The two traitors he let forth go
With wives and with their children too.
The cry arose all o'er the city,
And they laid on without pity.
Night and day the folk they slayeth;
All that they found were put to death.
Sister and son, mother and father;
They slew the children in the cader. *cradle*
All they bled, swain and knave;
Men and women that went with stave,

Old blind men, and all such,
And cripples that walked with crutch.

Five days five nights, through and through,
They slew folk in that borough.

There was shed so much blood
That man and horse to the knees yode.

How King Priam and his daughter Dame Polyxena were cruelly slain by young Pyrrhus

AND when they had slain them so
—A hundred thousand men and more—
Then spake Priam, of Troy the King,
When he stood in his tower and saw this thing:
"Alas!" he said. "With foul treason
Now have I lost my fair town!"
And said, "Alas that I was born:
Through treason we are all forlorn!
Had truth been amongst us all,
Troy had ne'er this chance befall.
Truth would have with right and law
That all traitors should be to-drawn;
Truth certain is laid down today,
And treason up-reared, wellaway!
Lived Hector my son or Paris,
Were it not than it now is.
Now have I no friend me to wreak;
Alas, why will my heart not break?
Now is the King of Greece today
The Lord of Troy, wellaway!
This had I wished ne'er to see,
That mine enemy e'er should be!"
The king wept for such untruth;
To see old men weep it is great ruth.
For the care and sorrow he saw that day
He fell to ground and in swooning lay.

His barons defended his tower fast
With great stones and arbalest;
The men of Greece the tower assailed
—Armèd well in hauberks of mail—
And assailed the tower fast,
And in they breaken at the last.[*]
All that they found they have slew,
And to the king they did go,
And hew the king to pieces small,
And the queen and her maidens all—
For them must be no ransom,
Not for king nor for baron.
    Pyrrhus taketh Polyxene,
The king's daughter, bright and sheen.
"My father," he said, "Sir Achilles,
For thy love slain he was,
In the temple with great treason;
For thee shall be no ransom."
She cried mercy and was full woe;
With his fist he smote her neck a-two.
He would not her slay with no weapon of steel;[†]
Thus he avenged his father well.[58]

Of the restoration of Queen Helen and the Returns of the Greeks

THE Queen of Greece they found that day
And brought her to Sir Menelae;
And they brought her before her lord,

[*] Harl. 525: "Knights defended the tower fast / But Neoptolemus breaketh in at the last"

[†] Harl. 525: "That a-two her neck he break / And all her kin he slew eke" *also*

And kissèd both with good accord.
The king made merry with his chivalry
When he had won the mastery.
He dwelt in Troy with his host
A month and more with mickle boast;
A season in Troy the king did take,
And mickle mirth and joy they make.
And when they liked to dwell no more
They dight their ships with sail and oar,*
And charged their ships with mickle goods
And sailed o'er the salty flood.
The folk of Greece of many a town
Came with carols and processìon,
And welcomed them in all things;
Sir Menelaus their king,
And Dame Helen his good wife—
For her was wakened mickle strife.[59]
There was joy in every town
Of the earls, and of barons;
Forty days the king held feast
That was both rich and honest
Of peacocks, pheasants, and bittern.
There was venison of hart, and boar;
There was pyment of claret too. *a type of mead*
To rich men and their retinue
There was made a rich service—
As rich as man e'er might devise.
And when the feast came to ending
They took their leave of the king,
And each man went to his country
And made joy with his company.

* Harl. 525: "They dight two hundred ships with oar"

Thus was ended the Battle of Troy;
God give us all heavenly joy.
Such a battle as it was one
Shall never be, nor shall be none.

And give all Christian souls good rest,
And ours when we come to that feast.
And that it may forever be
Say all "Amen!" for charity.

Explicit the Seege of Troye

THE RAWLINSON PROSE SIEGE OF TROY

THE RAWLINSON PROSE SIEGE OF TROY

Here beginneth the Sege of Troye.

Of Aeson and his brother Pelias, and how Pelias sent his nephew Jason in search of the Golden Fleece

AS THE noble and worthy clerk Guido writeth in his book[1] and declareth—and so doth the famous clerk Dares also—some time in Thessaly there was a king called Aeson. This king wished not in his young and lusty days to take any wife, but at the last was so far grown in age that his wits were not most perfect nor right reasonable for to rule and govern his realm nor his people, but he was fallen in a manner of dotage for age. For this cause he resigned both crown and sceptre with whole estate royal to his brother called Pelias.

But as clerks say, afterwards by enchantment and craft of medicine he was restored again to youth and lustiness, and took to wife one Medea. Upon Medea he got a son that was called Jason,[2] that when he drew to a certain age was committed to the rule and governance of his uncle Pelias. This Jason, by process of years, was held so noble and worthy of hand that his name sprung so wide and far that every man had great joy to hear speak of his worthiness and of his person.

Pelias, adverting and casting in his mind how himself and his issue might possess and enjoy the crown and dignity perpetually, and to exclude his nephew Jason forever, compassed full many a diverse way in his mind to the confusion and destruction of his said cousin. He held his nephew up always with fair flattery, and showed whole love outward where there was full deadly hate inward.

Upon a day, in the presence of all of his barons, he said to him in this wise: "Nephew Jason, thy great renown and worthiness sprung so wide in every country causeth me every heavenly and earthly joy. But Jason, for to have thy worthiness sprung wider, and more largely and openly to be known—and as a conqueror forever to be dreaded in every country—I have found a way, trusting fully that through thy manhood it shall be well achieved within short time."

Full desirous of manhood and worthiness, Jason thanked greatly his uncle, and prayed him to let him have knowledge thereof so that with his support and labour he might thereby increase and further his name.

Pelias, conceiving well his courage and manhood, said to him in this wise: "Cousin, it is openly known in many a land that within the Isle of Colchis there is a ram that beareth a Fleece of Gold which is of more worth then any man can tell. And if thou, by thy might and manhood might win and conquer that ram, thy renown and name shall spring up to heaven as the worthiest forever to be put in remembrance."

Jason, filled with knightly courage, was innocent of the fair and false treason compassed against him by the flattery of his uncle. Without the advice of any man he thus undertook this perilous enterprise, the which was fully imagined and purposed for his destruction and end, and prayed his uncle to ordain for him in all haste men and array as befitting his estate.

Trusting fully it should be Jason's confusion and end, Pelias was full joyful in heart, and let make in all haste possible a ship ready for him. As Guido sayeth, it was the fairest ship that ever sailed upon the water from land to land. The governor thereof was the wise and ready Philoctetes that had ready knowledge and inspection of every storm or tempest appearing in the sky, and also of star, stone, and needle.

How Jason and Hercules were summarily ejected from the coast of Phrygia by Laomedon, King of Troy

JASON, also having with him in his vessel as his fellow the strong and mighty Hercules with many another lusty and manly man of Greece—with full leave taken of his uncle—was under sail, full worthily taking his journey. He was sailing on the salt sea toward the Isle of Colchis when a tempest suddenly arose and so hurled and laboured the ship until he was driven into the Isle of Troy, whereof Jason and his fellowship were right fain of any succour of the land for to have some ease and rest after their perilous labour on the sea.

King Laomedon, being in his city of Troy, was informed of malice that there was a ship stuffed with men of war arrived in his land out of Greece. Supposing they had come to do some malice against him or his people, he anon sent messengers to Jason and said to him in this wise: "Forasmuch as ye that be strangers be arrived here, in guise of war without licence or safe conduit, the king chargeth you that in all haste ye remove from his ground—for if ye disobey and keep not his commandment ye be of too feeble power to resist and to withstand his will of you. Wherefore we counsel you to void in haste."

Jason and Hercules, hearing his message from the king, were somedeal aggrieved in heart, and answered in this wise: "Sirs, since it is the king's lust that we so suddenly shall depart, we shall not long sojourn here. But of ill-fortune we be driven hither despite our lust—we had supposed that the king, of his goodness, would rather have sent for us strangers to have somedeal refreshed us than in this wise to banish us hence, thinking him nor none of his harm in good faith! I pray you to say to him on our part that since we find his kindness so strange to us at this time, and he will not suffer us in no wise to rest on his land, once ere this day three years—if Fortune will suffer—we shall arrive somewhat near him without licence, safe conduit, or protection of him or any of his; yea, and in such wise that it shall not be in his might nor power to resist nor let our arrival nor tarrying, while us best list!"[3]

Of Jason's arrival at Colchis, and how by the aid of Medea he won the Golden Fleece

THUS took they their leave and went straight to ship, and had wind at will until they came to the haven of Colchis. Upon their arrival Aeëtes, king of that land, came himself in right gentle wise and brought them into Jaconites, his city where his palace was.[4] For that time Aeëtes made all the disport[*] and cheer that might be done, charging all manner of officers to attend about them so that they lacked nothing that may have been to their pleasance. He bid also the fair Medea—his daughter and heir[5]—to do all the disport and cheer to Jason and his fellowship that she could or might in performing of her father's will.

This Medea, as Guido writeth, was passing any other as well of beauty as of person as of cunning, nurture, and knowing of all the sciences, nigromancy,[†] magic, sorcery, and other enchantments that now be forbidden. She advised always the person of Jason, considering his worthy birth of blood royal and his great renown and name of worthiness praised in many a land, and hath taken to full purpose to find the means and ways—if Fortune would—for to be his wife, taking no reward to father, heritage, nor other worldly riches.

Within short time she found a time, place, and leisure to the execution of her intent; first inquiring of him of his blood and birth, afterward of his causes and journeys into that country. To this he always made his answer, and told her the truth of all that she asked him, and of the enterprise that he had taken on hand. To Jason she gave answer in manner as one that had lost her franchise, and in a manner stood under his power—and he innocent and not knowing thereof—saying to him in this wise:

"It is good that one so noble and worthy as ye be right well advised while ye stand at large to take upon you so importable a

[*] Play or relaxation

[†] Black magic

charge—the which is unlikely and impossible for any earthly man for to achieve. For truly in that case there may no manhood avail, and armour and weapon serve for naught; for ere that ye come to the ram, ye must fight with two bulls of brass, each casting out at the mouth fire and flame that will burn and consume any earthly matter. These bulls ye must in such wise overcome that ye shall take them by the horns, and so lead them to the yoke and plough the land with their labour. This done and overcome in such wise, ye shall meet and fight with a dragon—in manner of a serpent—whose venom is so contagious that there may no manner of metal abide the malice thereof. The breath of it is worse than any pestilence, and there may no weapon made of matter perish the scales. This overcome and done, ye shall come to the ram, which is without defence or resistance. But for to attain so far, it is impossible for any earthly man."

Jason, remembering well every word and peril, stood somedeal astounded of himself, and answering again he said: "Truly, my lady Medea, of your gentle warning and counsel I thank you as your own man in all that I can or may. But truly, since that I have so farforth taken on this enterprise, I shall do my full business and power to achieve it if Fortune will assent; for I would rather end and die with worship than endure and leave in reproof and shame. For then might every man say that Jason had undertaken an enterprise which for cowardice he durst not hold nor complete."

Medea, seeing his manful courage, rejoiced greatly within her heart, and said to him in this wise: "Right worthy Jason, since ye list in no wise to leave your journey for the great worthiness and manhood that I have heard of you, so that ye will be ensured to me to be ruled and governed after me, I trust verily to show you such means and ways that ye shall achieve your purpose—and truly without me ye may never have your intent in that matter."

To whom Jason answered and said that truly with heart and will he would be ruled as she list to govern him. Whereof she, right fain and glad, found a place and time at more leisure to inform him.

The night next following, she, having a woman of her assent, sent privily and unaware of any man after Jason, who was right glad and fain to obey her will and come to her chamber. Medea—also fain of his coming—set him down on her bedside and anon unclosed a little coffer and brought before him a little image of gold, whereupon she made him to swear that he should follow her intent and will in all things. Jason, always desiring to fulfil and achieve his purpose, followed her will and lust in all things.

This oath and assurance made, she said to him: "Jason, ye know well that I am daughter and heir to the king my father, and I desire no other thing for my labour in saving of your life and worship but that ye would take me before all others."

Jason, thinking on her noble birth, great beauty, and worthy estate, granted thereto with full glad cheer and heart, and they were thereupon ensured on the new.*

Then she took him a little image of gold that he should bear privily on him, the which was a secure defence against any spirit. Also she anointed his body all over with a precious ointment that was a noble defence against all manner of venom. She took him also a vial with an ointment for to cast in the throats of the bulls when they gaped upon him, which would englue their jaws together and bereave them of their might. Also she took him a ring with a stone called Agate, which would cause him to be invisible so neither bull nor dragon should have no sight of him. She took to him also a written charm, that first when he came to the sight of the fiends he should kneel with good devotion and say.

All these things received and taught, he took his leave of Medea, and went to her father for his license to go toward his journey.

The king, seeing his manly courage, said to him: "Jason, be right well advised ere that ye proceed any further in your journey. Consider well that it is impossible for any man to achieve that purpose.

* Sworn on the new moon (?)

Therefore my counsel is that ye cease thereof; for I take all the gods to record and witness that it is not my will that ye should so put your body in adventure to be spilt, of which truly I am right sorry."

Notwithstanding all the sermoning, Jason and Hercules, with all their lusty company, took their leave and went straight to boat, rowing forth into a little isle where the ram with the Fleece of Gold was in keeping. Jason entered into the land alone, leaving Hercules with all his people within the boat, and charging them to abide there still unto the time that he come again. He took his passage full manly unto the time that he came to the sight of the dreadful bulls, where anon kneeling on his knees he said the charm as he was taught and arose up, taking his pace toward the bulls, which with horrible and grisly gaping cast out fire and flame. Jason full wisely and manly took his vial with his liquor and boldly cast it into their throats, wherewith all suddenly their jaws englued together so that all their might and power failed and ceased. Jason full boldly took them by the horns; they inclined and obeyed his lust to the yoke and plough, and tilled the land as patiently as any other beast.

That enterprise done, he took his way straight to the dragon, which anon cast out such an air with venom that would infect all a country. Holding his ring on his hand, Jason went straight to him, and anon the dragon lost sight, power, and might. Jason took his sword and by good leisure smote off his head, and anon rased* all the teeth out of his head and cast them on the land that he had ploughed with the bulls. Of this cursed seed sprang up anon through the might of the Devil armed men, of which every one slew the other anon in that tide.

That so done, he went straight to the ram, which made no defence against him. He took it by the horns and with a knife cut its throat, and so at his own leisure flayed off its rich skin. This he took with him, and went to his boat where Hercules with his men was abiding upon his coming, the which were right glad and joyful to see him

* Extracted by the root

safe of body. During all this time Medea, being in a high tower, saw him from point to point; how he performed his enterprise, always praying to her gods for his good speed.

Jason, entering his boat with his Fleece and fellowship, returned again to King Aeëtes—the which was right sorry that Jason had won so the Fleece (but always made him fair cheer outward). But some clerks say that King Aeëtes let make the bulls and dragon in so horrible wise by craft of nigromancy to keep his great treasure.

But for that worthy conquest Jason was renowned and named the worthiest conqueror in any land. All the court and people came running for to marvel and wonder upon the Golden Fleece, every man saying his advice thereupon.

The night following his coming again, Medea—being in her chamber alone—sent privily after Jason. With full heart and will he came to her unaware of any person, telling her everything of his journey—of which she was right glad and joyful—so that he lasted within her chamber all that night. Between them two they found a time and leisure for to steal away by night into Greece with the Fleece of Gold, and all the treasure of the king her father—which was to the confusion of Medea, for afterward he left her in great mischief and took another lady. And he had by Medea two sons, and because they were so like Jason, Medea slew hem both.[6]

But of her I speak no more at this time.

How at Pelias' bidding, Hercules and his comrades sacked and destroyed the city of Troy

AND when Jason and Hercules were come to Greece, Pelias—to all men's sight—made them the greatest cheer that ever man might, but in heart it was the contrary. Jason told Pelias his uncle of all his adventures, whereof he made him full joyful, and told him also how he was "in a tempest driven into Troy, where King Laomedon sent anon, charging us to void his land on pain of death—which was to us a full great discomfit after our great labour in the sea. Whereupon we made our great oaths, and by his messengers sent him word that ere three years were passed we would arrive a little near him to his disease and harm—if that we might. Wherefore we pray you, Uncle, of your good help and succour in this matter."

Pelias anon with good heart granted their desire, saying that he would go himself with them in that journey.[7] He sent Hercules to his cousin Telamon, King of Messene,[8] with certain letters and tokens that he should come with all that he might get, and sent him also to the two worthy kings and brethren Castor and Pollux—Kings of Sparta and brethren also to Helen, Queen of Tyndaris[9]—and also to the Duke of Pylos[*] that was lord of the great province of Greece. And all with good will granted Pelias' desire to go with him to Troy.

Pelias in all haste possible made his retinue, and with all these worthy lords mustered in a fair green plain—which was a huge multitude of people. Taking their ships they had weather and wind at will until they came to the royal haven called Simoent or Tenedos,[10] right nigh the noble city of Troy, which they took within the night.

Pelias anon assembled his lords together, and said to them in this wise: "Sirs, ye know the cause of our coming hither and for what purpose, and think well that Laomedon is right manly and wise and cruel of hand. Wherefore, unless we prove well our manhood our name is lost forever."

Hercules, answering again said: "If ye will be ruled by mine advice and counsel, I trust fully to achieve our purpose." To whom they granted everyone to be ruled. "Then my counsel is that King Castor take with him a sufficient fellowship and be put out before, showing him openly before the city with banners displayed; King Telamon with another fellowship privily as it were in an ambush if need be to succour; and Pelias with all his people abiding here still. And if it need, to be

[*] Nestor

succour and rescue to them both, Jason and I with another army—all privily ere the day spring—shall lay us under the vines below the walls of the city, so that when Laomedon skirmishes with you we shall fall between them and the town. And so between you and us we may take and slay him—and peradventure* win the town also, that is so richly stuffed with all manner of treasure, wherewith we may freight all our ships and lead into Greece."

All the lords, thinking his counsel good, followed his intent.

Castor in the morning showed him openly before the city, with banners displayed in the field in the sight of Laomedon and all the citizens of Troy. Anon Laomedon assembled his people and with manly courage issued out at the gates, meeting with Castor, and in such wise skirmished with him that he slew a great part of his people. Had not Telamon come then quickly with succour he would have slain Castor, but Telamon broke so suddenly upon Laomedon that he slew a great many people of Troy. But always they of the city issued out, and at the last put Telamon and Castor to discomfit.

Then Pelias broke out with a fierce company, skirmishing full long time with the Trojans, and full much people on both parties were slain. Then broke out Jason and Hercules suddenly in the back of the Trojans, that so between Hercules and the Greeks the Trojans were slain and discomfited. Jason kept still the gates of the city, where they smote off the head of Laomedon and cast it under the horses' feet, slaying all the remnant.[11]

And so they passed into the city, where they left alive neither man, woman, nor child. The Greeks despoiled all the city of its riches and treasure, stuffing full their ships therewith, and preserving Hesione daughter of King Laomedon alive because of her beauty. But they cast down the city and left no stone standing upon other, but made it plain even with the soil.

* Perhaps

How Priamus, son of King Laomedon, rebuilt the city of Troy

THIS vengeance so cruelly done, they took to their ships, leading Hesione with all other treasure with them into Greece. At this time was Priamus—son and heir to King Laomedon—lying at the siege before a castle, whither tidings came to him of all this strong vengeance.[12] He, all troubled and amazed of all these sorrowful tidings, suddenly left the siege and came home, where he found no stone standing upon other, but all laid plain with the earth. For sorrow of which, as well for father, sister, and other friends, and for all the other harm, despite, and shame, he took such a heaviness that for a long time he was out of himself.

But by process of time, with comfort of friends he was drawn to sadness again. And anon thereafter he took to full purpose to re-edify and build the city of new, and in such wise that it should not so lightly be lost. In all haste Priamus sent into many a country and diverse land for the most prudent and wisest men of craft that might be found and got—sparing for no cost nor expense—purposing fully to make such a city and so strong that he would never dread for no enemy: neither for war nor peace. And so there came full many a crafty mason, carpenter, smith, and all others that belong to such occupation that had full ready knowledge and cunning as well in geometry as in other subtle insight of works. They took their marks and measures of length and compass of the city, the which was made so large that a great river ran through the midst. Upon this river was set many a mill and stuff of fish enough within the same, along with all manner of corns and fruits growing within the city; pastures, wood, and meadow, so that they should never need of nothing without.

For as Guido sayeth, it was three days' journey about the walls, the which were raised eighty cubits of height, and towered so thick that every tower might succour the other, with every tower sixty cubits higher than the walls. And both walls and towers were fully machicolated,* with deep ditches, and full mighty countermured† so that if any man were within he might never out without help. In this city was set six gates, of which the first hight Dardanian, the second Thymbraean, the third Ilian, the fourth Scaean, the fifth Antenorean, and the sixth Trojan. And before every one of these was set a strong bulwark as mighty as any castle, with bars and hips for a sure defence. There were also many small posterns with planchettes,‡ if need were to issue out as well in time of peace as of war. He let make also by the one side of the town a huge and a mighty donjon: a tower that was so high and thick that no ordinance should hurt it, diched and countermured strongly, within which Priamus held his palace, and it was called Ilion.[13] He let make also his worthy temple of his gods full richly arrayed, where he made his rites and sacrifices.

This city fully made and performed, Priamus sent into many a land and town for the most subtle men of all manner of crafts that might be got and found, giving them both house and land free as for their own lives. He set every craft by themselves, staffing the city also with labourers and commoners for to labour and plough. He sent also into many a country for the manliest men of war that might be got, staffing every tower about the city with them to defend the city if need were, and assigning to every tower a portion of livelihood for their wages eternally to endure. Within the city there was all manner of commodities so that they need nothing to seek without while the world may endure—neither for man nor beast.

This city so worthily made and staffed, Priamus full royally dwelt in its walls with Hecuba his Queen, having about them their children Hector, Paris, Deiphobus, Helenus that was a noble clerk, Troilus,

* Having an overhanging parapet, through which stones can be dropped or arrows shot onto besiegers

† Having a double row of walls

‡ A small plank, presumably set in place to provide temporary egress from the postern

Polydorus, and Ganymede that died;[14] of daughters Creusa that was married to Aeneas, Cassandra (a full great divineress), and Polyxena, and also of other sons begotten on purchase*—thirty full-worthy knights.

How Antenor was sent into Greece to regain Hesione, and of his failure to achieve his purpose

PRIAMUS, thus being in his great ease and wealth, remembered him upon a day on the great cruelty done to him; he called his lords every one, and said to them in this wise: "Sirs, ye know well of the great vengeance and cruelty done to our ancestors and destruction of our city and treasure by the Greeks, and of the taking and ravishing of my sister Hesione that is yet held and used of King Telamon to her open and great slander and shame—and ours also, the which grieveth me more than all the other harms. Wherefore, by your good advice and counsel, I am fully purposed for to send unto the Greeks to wit whether they will reform and amend any of these great wrongs or no."

To which purpose all the lords consented, and said it were well done to assay their will therein.

Then, forasmuch as Antenor was named and known for the most prudent and wisest man of all that country and in many another land also, Priamus sent him upon his embassy into Greece unto Pelias, to whom he said in this wise: "Priamus, King of Troy, would that ye remember on the great wrong and vengeable cruelty done to King Laomedon his father and to his city of Troy, and prayed somedeal to amend and reform his great wrong and destruction and taking away of all their treasure—and in especial the withholding so long of his sister Hesione, to his great shame and all her kin and friends."

To this Pelias answered and said: "If that Priamus holds him

* Illegitimate

grieved or displeased of anything done by us before this time, say to him that he take amends therefore where that he may—for truly of us get he naught!"

Seeing that it was no bote to tarry there no longer, Antenor went straight to King Telamon. On Priamus' behalf he prayed him to restore again his sister Hesione that he had so long both used and occupied, taking no reward of her birth nor of the gods.

Telamon gave answer and said: "Say to Priamus that against his will and lust I brought her hither, and at his desire I will never send her again—and for his sake she shall fare the worse!"

Antenor, having his answer, went straight to Castor and Pollux, praying them on Priamus' behalf somewhat for to make restitution of the great wrongs and harms done to them, to his father, and to others of Troy. Castor and Pollux gave answer and said that if Priamus held him "displeased for our deeds done at Troy before this time, bid him hold him well thereto, lest he take more hereafter if he noise it too much!"

Antenor, having these final answers, took his ship and returned to Troy, and made full report of all their answers.

Priamus, right greatly moved of these answers, called before him Hector and all his sons with all his other lords. He made Antenor declare to them all the crooked answers, whereof they were all grievèd sore.

Of the Rape of Helen by Paris

PRIAMUS, calling his son Hector, said to him: "Forasmuch as the Greeks have done us these great wrongs and harms, and also eternal shame in the taking and yet withholding of thine aunt Hesione, for all this have I but short answer: I am advised to ordain a retinue of manly and worthy men, and to send them thither with thee as their captain for to be avenged upon the Greeks and bring from thence Hesione, thine aunt."

Hector, answering his father, said: "It is well done to be well advised ere ye send in such wise thither, and to take so great a purpose and enterprise into such a land as Greece is. It were good to think on the end, for the shame of my aunt is much less than the loss of many a thousand lives."

His brother Paris, hearing him say these words, said unto his father: "If it pleases you to let me have a retinue, I will undertake to fetch home my aunt—else I will do them as great a shame ere that I depart from thence."[15]

Hector, answering his brother, said: "Brother, it is good to be well advised, for all the might of Europe and Africa be allied and under subjection to Greece—and many another mighty region. To us is neither help nor succour belonging, save only the province of Asia, which is right simple against all our enemies."

Paris, taking no reward to the words of Hector nor to nothing that followed, hath fully taken his purpose—the journey—upon him, praying his father that people and shipping might be ready in haste, along with such stuff needed there pertaining and belonging to his estate.

Of Paris' enterprise and courageous will his father the king was right glad and fain, and in all haste sent into all the parts of his land for the best and manliest men that he might find to make up his retinue. Priamus ordained ships and all other stuff that should belong to him, so that it was all ready; as well stuffed of victuals as other ordinance for the war—both for water and for land.

Mustering his people, Paris took leave and blessing of father and mother and went to ship. Having weather and wind at will, he arrived in an isle of Greece called Cythera, of which the worthy King Menelaus was lord, who of fortune at that time was from home, for a title that he claimed in Thessaly.[16] In this isle there was a temple of Diana the great goddess, at the which time the great solemnity and vigil of the said goddess was being held.[17] To the sacrifices and offering all the people of the country about had come thither for to do their old customs and duties. To this temple also came Paris with a certain man of his fellowship, for to see the visage of that country.

Fair Helen—queen and wife to King Menelaus—heard of the coming of Paris into the temple, and came with a certain number of her maidens privily to have a sight of that young, lusty Paris. She took her place on the one side of the temple where Paris with one of his fellowship made his walk and stations, casting always his eye and sight privily toward the fair Helen—who suddenly was so planted in his heart that all other business was forgotten and laid aside.

Helen, being in her closet and seeing this fresh, lusty Paris so well demeanoured in his array, walking always beside to and fro, suddenly was so set in her heart that all other things she forgot. She strove with herself how to find a means for to be in speech with him; Paris in likewise tormented in his mind how to find a way to come to her presence. Among these burning thoughts he suddenly left his fellow and went straight into the closet of Helen, whereof she was the gladdest woman alive, having him in her presence. These two held them so long together in the temple that either had full knowledge of other's heart, where there was no joy to seek. At this time it was fully appointed and accorded between them two that she should go with Paris to Troy. Thus they set their time and hour of their going.

Taking his leave of her, Paris went straight unto his ship, charging all his people in their best array to wait upon him, and also his shipmen that his ship were under sail.

In the point of the day Paris with his fellowship took his way again to the temple, taking Helen by the hand and despoiling the temple of all the jewels and relics found therein. He held his way straight unto the palace of King Menelaus, robbing, despoiling, and taking away with him all the riches and treasure found there within, carrying it to the ships with all the other riches and goods found within the isle. Helen and he with all their fellowship entered their vessels, drew up sail, and with wind at will went their way, holding the high sea until they came to the lands of Troy unto an isle called Tenedos. Here they landed and rested them, Paris sending to his father King Priamus certifying him wholly as it was fortuned.

Priamus was full glad in heart for the taking of Helen, trusting by her to have had again his sister, but it turned afterward to much more mischief on both parties. Taking with him Hector, Troilus, and all his other children and lords, Priamus came to the isle of Tenedos where Paris, Helen, and all their other fellowship were abiding his will. Priamus anon let array and ordain the marriage between Paris and Helen, after which they anon conveyed her full royally into Troy where they began their full lusty life.

How the Greeks, at Menelaus' bidding, collected a fleet and sailed against Troy

AFTER the ravishing of Helen, the great noise arose suddenly throughout the isle of Cythera and so through all the land of Greece, unto the time that it came to the ears of King Menelaus where he was in a strange country—for sorrow of which he fell in such a sudden rage that he had nigh destroyed himself. But as soon as he might appease his mortal sorrow he returned home into Cythera where he found his palace, the temple, and all the isle about clean despoiled of all the riches, treasure, and other goods that were within; the which in such wise renewed his sorrows that he was nigh fallen into despair.

But by process of time, with great comfort and labour of friends, he was repaired to his wisdom and sadness. He sent in all haste unto Castor and Pollux—brethren of Queen Helen—that must be chief for the pursuit of her, and sent also unto all the friends that they might get in any country to be avenged on the Trojans.[18]

The Greeks, holding themselves so royal and worthy, had full great despite that any Trojan should be so hardy to do such great outrage and shame within their lands. Whereupon they took fully to purpose—every lord at his own cost and charge—to be avenged of that great despite in all the haste possible.

They came to King Menelaus in this wise:[19] first the worthy Achilles; Diomedes; King Tendalus; the worthy King Agamemnon that was made governor of the Greek host; King Patroclus; King Oileus; King Ajax; King Telamon; Ulysses; King Protesilaus; Neoptolemus; King Palamedes; King Podalirius; Machaon; the King of Persia; the King of Syme; Antiphus and Phidippus; Machaon and Podalirius;[20] Duke Antiphus of Elis and Euryalus; Philoctetes; Agapenor, King of Arcadia; Treorius, King of Beysa; the King of Barbary; Mopsus, the King of Colophon; the King Pirus of Thrace; Duke Antiphus and Duke Phorcys of the isle of Boetine; King Pylaemenes of Tigris; King Perses; King Sigamon with his two brethren of Ethiopia; Rhesus, King of Thrace; Archilochus; King Epistrophus. All these kings each brought a great number of ships stuffed sufficiently in the most mighty wise as well of men as of victuals, beside many another lord that came at the desire of these said lords to be avenged upon the Trojans.

The king Priamus, having knowledge of this great purpose taken against him in so fervent wise, ordained full manly and wisely by the counsel of Hector to resist their malice in stuffing the city with victuals. He ordained so great a number of men of war that he had of kings, dukes, and other great lords of name three hundred and thirteen, bringing with them five hundred and fourteen thousand beside all other stuff of the city, repairing full strongly all the defences of Troy.

The Greeks assembled and mustered all their mighty and huge power in a day upon a fair plain, which was full marvellous to behold; then anon was ordained every man to bear harness to ship, and every captain their vessels assigned. Drawing up anchor and sail, and having weather and wind at will, in a whole fleet they sailed together unto the time that they came within the lands of Troy, into the haven of Simoent.[21]

Of the various battles between the Greeks and the Trojans, and of the prowess of Hector

KING Priamus, having full knowledge of the Greeks' landing, purposed fully to prevent their arrival, and ordained Hector, Paris, and Troilus with great number of people to hinder them if they might.

The Greeks, having knowledge of their purpose against them, purveyed their landing in full wise array and good ordinance in salvation of themselves. Notwithstanding which, Hector with his fellowship gave them such battle at their landing that there was slain on the Greeks' part twenty-three thousand and four hundred men. And Hector himself there slew King Protesilaus and more than a thousand men with his own hand before returning again to Troy.

All that night the Greeks came in to land, and in the point of the day they came in whole battle before the city with so great a multitude of people that they made seventeen great wards with full mighty ordinance in each. And chief captain and chieftain of all the Greeks' part during the siege was King Agamemnon, and on the Trojans' part was Hector chosen.

Having espied of their coming that morning before Troy, Hector, ordaining a certain number of people with him, met them in the field. They skirmished together until dark night, where Hector himself slew two kings,[22] and great part were slain on both parties—but the more part on the Grecian side. After this day there was daily skirmishing during eight months and great slaughter on both parties, and namely on the Greeks' part.

After this fervent war was taken a treaty enduring forty days for to relieve men hurt on both sides.

Following the truce, Hector ordained upon on day with him his brethren Paris, Troilus, and Deiphobus, with a great number of people to fight with them, during which skirmish was slain thirty thousand and seven hundred on both parties. And there was Deiphobus slain, and on the Greeks' part King Archilochus, Patroclus, and King Antiphus,[23] but always the Greeks turned home at night with the worse. This skirmishing engendered so great hate and envy on both parties that they skirmished and fought daily together without any speech of treaty two years and three months, within which term was great multitude slain on both sides, but principally on the Greeks' side.

King Agamemnon, seeing the great mischief and loss of people, sent into Troy to Priamus for a treaty that endured six months, within the which either party had their disport with other—as well the Greeks into the city as the Trojans among the Greeks.

Under this treaty Calchas of Troy—a bishop, a great clerk, and a diviner—found by his calculation and by the answer of his gods that Troy should be destroyed within a short time. Taking fully to purpose to leave the Trojans and go to the Greeks, he was full worthily and nobly received of the Greeks for his great name and fame.[24] The Greeks purposed to give him a rule and governance among them, trusting within short time by his wisdom to achieve their purpose against Troy. For by his high wisdom and answer of his gods, and also because he knew all the counsel of Troy, he would the swifter bring it to confusion. And so by his false sleights and untrue wiles they did and performed.

After the treaty had ended there began a new, fervent war, the armies skirmishing daily together, that full great and huge numbers were slain on both parties. It fortuned upon a day that Hector came proudly skirmishing with them from morrow until dark night. On this day the Trojans had the worse, for there was slain King Epistrophus and King Diores,[25] and Antenor—a full famous lord and chief counsellor of Troy—was taken with many another worthy lord. Because of this they resorted daily to so fervent and mortal war that it endured eighteen months without any speech of treaty, so that the people on both parties were greatly diminished and lost. But on the Greeks' part they were oft refreshed, and on Troy's part no succour, but ever they wasted.

It fortuned that at the Greeks' request there was another treaty taken that endured three months, during which either party came to and fro to the other, disporting and playing with each other. Under this treaty the false traitor Calchas—that was made chief counsellor on the Greeks' part—came into their council among the lords, praying them that forasmuch that he was of his own volition come to them, leaving behind him all the goods and namely his child and daughter Cressida, that they would give him some prisoner of Troy by the which he might have out his daughter from the Trojans.

To Calchas the Greeks granted anon and gave him the famous man Antenor, that was one of the chief counsellors of Troy before—by whom afterward was the city destroyed and lost, for where that Priamus sent out Cressida to fetch home Antenor, he was after traitor to him and to the city.[26]

Of Hector's death, by Achilles slain, and of the marvellous manner in which his body was embalmed

THE time of treaty ended, Hector, purposing him to made a proud journey upon the Greeks, ordained him five wards—each one to succour the other. The night before the wife of Hector, lying in her bed, had a vision in her sleep by which she understood well that if Hector held his purpose the morrow in the field that he should be slain. Whereupon she came running to him, praying him as for that day to abstain him from the field, and telling him of her vision. To this he said it was but false belief and idolatry, and set naught thereby, bidding her to speak no more thereof, for he would not break his purpose for nothing. She, running to Priamus, prayed him to restrain his purpose, informing him what should follow if he went out that day, and to let Paris and Troilus hold his purpose—the which with great pain obeyed his charge. Paris and Troilus skirmished in the field, and in short time were driven back toward the city, but with right great numbers slain on both parties.

Hector, in a manner seeing them discomfited, armed him in

haste, taking his horse and riding out at the gate. He returned the Trojans again into the field, encountering King Pirus, whom he slew with his spear.[27] Then came King Palamedes with a great multitude of people and fell upon Hector. To Palamedes Hector returned and put at discomfiture, and smote him down from his horse, alighting down for to take from him his coat—as was his usage when he had slain any lord. And as at that time he had none of his people about him, unaware behind him came Achilles and bore him through with a spear, whereby the flower of knighthood fell down dead to the ground.[28]

The noise sprung through the field that Hector was slain, for sorrow of which the Trojans, full of sorrow and care, anon returned again to the city carrying the body of Hector with them. For whom Priamus, Hecuba, Polyxena, Paris, Troilus, and all the city after made the greatest lamentation and deadly sorrow that with their lives might be made, falling fully in despair, and trusting no other but in short time to lose the city and all. For Hector was so noble of governance and so doughty of hand that he had slain with his own hand fifteen kings beside many another lord.[29] He never failed to put discomfit where he had the governance unto that time, which he might not escape, eschew, nor void—notwithstanding that he was warned before.

The Trojans sent out for a treaty of six months, during which Priamus, ordaining for the sepulchre of Hector, full royally held the obsequies and vigils. He brought therein the rich jewels, cloths of gold, incense, balms, milk, with many another rich thing, so that the savour was made sweet up to heaven—always conserving the body whole by craft of man to endure bodily right as he did before, saving that he was without life. And there was made a tomb; the most royal and rich that might be ordained, Hector standing thereupon in the flesh, holding his sword drawn in his hand.

And by craft there were ordained small pipes of gold put through his head, stretching through every vein and limb of his body. Through these pipes was running by craft a liquor into every part of his body, that always kept the body like fresh and green and well coloured.

Set also under his feet was a basin with a quantity of balm, which made his breath as sweet as ever it was, and a wind by craft from under his feet blew through him as though he had been quick and breathing, so that no stranger should well know but that he were alive. And of his array it were too long to tell.

How Achilles became enamoured of Polyxena, and refrained from battle with the Trojans

BUT under this treaty taken between the Trojans and the Greeks, after the royal tomb was made and done, either party came to disport with the other. Upon a day Achilles entered the city with the other Greeks in a poor soldier's array—unknown of the Trojans—for to see the guise and visage of them, holding his way straight into the temple where the obsequies and vigils were being done. Priamus, Hecuba, Paris, Troilus, with many another lord and lady were doing their sacrifices and observances, as their guise was, for Hector; him always beholding freshly and sternly on them, and namely—as to him it seemed—on Achilles, with sword drawn in hand. Whereof Achilles was astonished and abashed, standing in doubt whether he was quick or dead—saving he comforted himself with the mortal business that he saw there made for him.

Among the press Achilles cast his sight aside and saw the fair Polyxena, sister of Hector and Troilus, whose love anon pierced his hard, cursed heart in so strong a wise that he might not well endure his hard pains. Returning again to the Greeks with the greatest pain that might be suffered, he prayed a servant of his—a well-advised knight—to go unto Hecuba upon his behalf, desiring her daughter Polyxena in marriage. Hecuba, anon remembering on his worthiness and also of the mischief that was likely to follow if she denied his desire, said that she would speak thereof unto Priamus. Whereto Priamus answered and said that if Achilles would take upon him to make the Greeks cease their war—and also that he would be full friend to him and to all the Trojans as alliance asketh—he would grant his will therein.

Of this answer Achilles was the joyfullest man alive, promising fully to perform his desire. He took his way straight unto King Agamemnon where he was in council among his lords, giving them his advice and counsel that forasmuch as a great part of the people were destroyed, and how that their gods were displeased for the death of so huge a number that were slain on both parties (if the quarrel of the Greeks were done not of good but of pride he could not say), he gave them his counsel to return again to Greece ere Fortune turned fully against them.

To Achilles they gave answer and said since they had bid so long, and—as they trusted—were now at the point of winning of the city, they would not leave it so, but make all things ready for the field against the morrow because the treaty was done that day.[30]

On the morrow the Greeks ran before the city, and Troilus and Paris encountering them in the field slew on the Greeks' part great number and drove them home into their tents, despoiling and burning their lodgings. Achilles, holding him still, would in no wise fight against the Trojans for the love of fair Polyxena.[31]

How Troilus was slain by Achilles, and how Achilles, enticed within the temple, was there treacherously slain by Paris

ON THE next day following Troilus with his company came out proudly, skirmishing with the Greeks and slaying great numbers of them so that they flew into the tent of Achilles, which stood at defence against Troilus. The Greeks so retreated from Troilus that of fortune he slew King Phidippus and King Machaon,[32] and wounded Diomede through the body, following him so that his horse was slain. Troilus' people returned again, where Achilles with a great people fell on him and smote off his head, and drew the body after him at his horse's tail in the most shameful wise that ever any worthy man had without cause. For this Achilles was greatly reproved—as well of the Greeks as of the Trojans.[33] For sorrow of Troilus' death Priamus, Hecuba, and all the Trojans were greatly in despair, for after Hector he was their protector.

Hecuba, thinking on this great cruelty and false treason of Achilles, purposed fully by some treason to bring him to his end. She sent to her son Paris, and bade him ordain a fellowship ready to slay Achilles; for she would send for him as for the treaty of the marriage, bidding him meet with her in the temple, where she should keep him in secret wise until Paris saw the best time to fall on him and slay him.

Achilles was the gladdest man on the earth when he was sent for, trusting to have a full end of his marriage. Taking with him but one knight or two, he came unto the temple, and as he kneeled, one smote him under the foot whereof he died anon. And then they smote off his head, and cast the body into the canal where dogs and crows would devour him.[34]

Of the conspiracy of Antenor and Aeneas to surrender the city to the Greeks

AFTER which treason so done to Achilles, the Greeks so fervently warred upon the Trojans daily that great part was destroyed on both sides, but namely on the Trojans' part.

Upon a day Paris made him ready to make a journey on the Greeks, which in likewise made them ready to run before the city, and at the gates they met so fervently that there was great slaughter. But the Trojans had the worse, for Paris was there slain and great part of his people, which renewed the sorrow of Priamus for then had he no chieftain left alive to govern his people. Whereupon Priamus took to purpose to keep the city, and no more to issue out nor to skirmish with them.[35]

Antenor and Aeneas, purposing fully to have the city destroyed, came to Priamus saying in this wise: "It is needful to make a treaty for a peace, and to restore again Helen to her lord with treasure for his damage—such as might be accorded for."

Priamus, hearing their desires, denied their asking. Seeing this, the traitors went to all the common folk of the city, and with their speech so deceived them that they made all them come before the king, saying, "Unless if ye will consent to our desires, we will depose you and choose such a king as shall make a final peace for all our profit."

Priamus, saying how they had bent the common folk with false flattery such that he might not be of might to withstand all their malice, consented to a treaty for six months. Under this treaty the false traitors said that all the covenants should be engrossed and enrolled, and Helen delivered and Hesione brought again with deliverance of all the prisoners of either party, and so they should have eternal peace between the Greeks and the Trojans.[36]

How, by the introduction of a horse of brass into Troy, the city was destroyed and the royal prisoners slain

IN THE meantime Antenor and Aeneas, with the consent of the false traitor Calchas, let make a horse of brass so large and great that it was a marvel to speak thereof.[37] This horse the Greeks desired to offer to the goddess Minerva within the temple of Troy—like as they had made her avows before time—with Priamus granting as for their offering and sacrifice their intent. The horse, when it was by craft brought unto the gate, was so huge that it might not enter until the time that the walls were broken to make the gate larger. Within the horse was hidden a thousand armed men,[38] and the Greeks were also ready with every man in their best array, so that when the horse were passed through the postern gate then began men to leap out of its belly, and there they slew all that they found about the city as porters and keepers thereof. The Greeks, awaiting well upon them, ran in at once and so won the city.

Seeing this mischief, Priamus fled into the temple, where they found him and slew him. The Greeks despoiled the temple of all the riches and treasure (saving that which belonged to the two traitors), taking out Helen, and the son of Achilles slaying Polyxena, leaving no piece with other of her body.[39] Hecuba was led away into Greece to be stoned there to death, and breaking down the walls of the city, the Greeks slew all the people found therein, and burned every house.

Of the number of men slain on each side

BUT to tell of the debate and discord of the Greeks for the treasure in their going homeward, and how every lord slew other, and some were exiled forever out of Greece—as Dares and Guido wrote—it would make a long process. But from the laying of the siege unto the end were slain on the Greeks' part eight hundred thousand, seven hundred and sixteen men, and on the Trojans' part were slain six hundred thousand and nine hundred men.

And so, as I suppose, neither party won greatly at the end, for afterward Aeneas slew Antenor, so that he should not have greater rule than he among them that escaped out of Troy.[40] And the friends of Antenor banished and exiled Aeneas forever, where he lost all that ever he or his ancestors got. And always the end of every treason and falseness turneth to sorrow and mischief at the last.

Amen.

NOTES

THE SEEGE OF TROYE

1. Refers to Dares Phrygius, the fictional author of the *Excidio Trojae Historia* and wellspring of medieval Troy literature. He has been identified as a Trojan priest of Hephaestus mentioned in the *Iliad* when his son Phegus is slain by Diomedes (V.9-28)

2. Probably Menelaus, who is later described as the High King of Greece.

3. The poet of the *Seege of Troye* here makes King Laomedon of Troy the possessor of the Golden Fleece instead of King Aeëtes of Colchis (Apollonius of Rhodes, *Argonautica*, I.234-246).

4. In the *Argonautica* of Apollonius of Rhodes (c. 250 BC) the Argonauts do not land at Troy. This aligns with Apollodorus' *Bibliotheca*, in which Hercules rescues Laomedon's daughter Hesione from the sea monster during his twelve labours, and returns to sack Troy once his labours are complete, having been refused his due reward by Laomedon (*Bibliotheca*, II.5.9 & II.6.4). A lost *Argonautica* by mythographer Dionysius Scytobrachion—roughly contemporary with Apollonius of Rhodes—placed the rescue of Hesione within the voyage of the Argo; this version is summarised in the *Bibliotheca Historica* of Diodorus Siculus (IV.42.1-7), and also appears in the Latin *Argonautica* of Gaius Valerius Flaccus (II.451-578) (Galli, 2014, p. 137).

5. The *Seege of Troye* here diverges from Dares Phrygius, with the Argonauts' voyage to Colchis omitted. Dares reduces the journey and acquisition of the Golden Fleece to a single line, so it is unsurprising to see it culled altogether (*Excidio Trojae Historia*, 2).

6. The battle in MS. Harl. 525 plays out slightly differently in that Laomedon unhorses Hercules first, with Jason riding to the rescue.

7. The unnamed sons of Laomedon slain by Hercules appear in some medieval copies of Dares Phrygius' *Excidio Trojae Historia*, but are not present in the original.

8. Hesione was traditionally awarded to Telamon—not Hercules. According to Apollodorus, Hercules was enraged that Telamon had entered Troy

first, and drew his sword as if to slay him. Telamon at once began collecting stones, declaring that he was "building an altar to Hercules the Glorious Victor." Hercules was appeased, and awarded him Hesione when the siege was over (*Bibliotheca*, II.6.4).

9. According to Apollodorus, Priam (born "Podarces") was a child when Hercules sacked Troy; for this reason he was the only son of Laomedon to be taken prisoner rather than killed. When Hesione was given to Telamon as a prize, Hercules allowed her to choose one of the Trojan captives to go with her. When she chose Podarces, Hercules said that he must first be ransomed, so she took the veil from her head and gave it in exchange for her brother. From thenceforth he was named "Priam", from *priamai* ("to buy") (*Bibliotheca*, II.6.4).

10. The *Seege* poet names only three sons of Priam and one daughter (Polyxena). Classical sources gave him between fifty and seventy sons, and around twenty daughters (Apollodorus, *Bibliotheca*, III.12.5; Hyginus, *Fabulae*, 90). Sons Deiphobus and Helenus and daughter Cassandra—all three of whom are prominent in Dares Phrygius—are notably absent.

11. In MS. Harl. 525 he is sent away at birth.

12. MS. Lincoln's Inn does not specify the length of time Paris spent among the shepherds of Ida; Arundel XXII gives fifteen years, while Egerton 2862 has fourteen. If he was sent away at seven years old this would make him twenty-one or twenty-two upon his return to Troy, but only fifteen in Harl. 525 (see note 11).

13. This section on the early life of Paris comes from the lost work represented by the *Rawlinson Excidium Troiae*, which contains an account of his judging of the bulls. Its origin was a matter of fierce debate among early scholars of medieval Troy literature, with some theorising that it derived from a lost, expanded version of Benoît's *Roman de Troie*. The matter was settled in 1934 when American linguist E. Bagby Atwood presented his discovery of the *Excidium Troiae* in the Medieval Studies journal *Speculum*, although the text itself would not be published for another decade (Atwood, 1934, pp. 379-404).

14. The name "Paris" is actually thought to derive from the Greek *pēra* ("backpack" or "satchel"), in which the infant is said to have been placed by the herdsman Agelaus.

15. In MS. Harl. 525 they elect Hector. The other manuscripts follow Dares in sending Antenor (*Excidio Trojae Historia*, 4-5).

16. The *Seege of Troye* follows Dares Phrygius in presenting the Judgement of Paris as a dream (*Excidio Trojae Historia*, 7), although here the goddesses

Juno, Minerva and Venus, with the god Mercury as arbitrator become "Four ladies of Elven-Land": Saturnus, Jupiter, Mercurius and Venus. The episode becomes, in the words of M. E. Barnicle, "wholly Celtic and medieval" (Barnicle, 1927, p. xlvi), and divorced from its original association with the wedding of Peleus and Thetis.

17. This "ball" was of course an apple in the original myth (Apollodorus, *Bibliotheca*, E.3.2).

18. MS. Harl. 525 follows the traditional story, with the three goddesses quarrelling over a golden apple, although there is still no mention of the wedding of Peleus and Thetis.

19. Mohammed was often used by medieval writers and poets as a sort of "umbrella" deity for non-Christian characters. This can result in some bizarre situations—in this case we have a classical Graeco-Roman goddess apparently invoking a seventh-century Islamic prophet!

20. A verse seems to be missing here, with Pallas' offer to Paris omitted.

21. Menelaus is here presented as the High King of Greece, reigning in "Cytherion" (Cythera). He was traditionally the King of Sparta (Apollodorus, *Bibliotheca*, E.2.16), while Cythera was an island sacred to Venus, ruled by Sparta at various times in the classical period (Thucydides, IV.53.2). Dares Phrygius moves Paris' abduction of Helen from Sparta to Cythera (*Excidio Trojae Historia*, 10); the *Seege* poet goes one step further and moves Menelaus' entire seat of power to the island.

22. Refers to the semi-mythical "Alexander Romance"—a collection of apocryphal stories concerning Alexander the Great that was immensely popular in medieval Europe. According to the romance Alexander was fathered by the Egyptian pharaoh Nectanebo II, who seduced Queen Olympias of Macedon by disguising himself as the god Ammon (Anonymous, *Kyng Alisaunder*, ll.235-456).

23. This is a rare instance of the *Seege of Troye* being closer to the Greek Epic Cycle than Dares Phrygius. In the *Excidio*, Menelaus is away from home when Paris arrives in Sparta—their ships actually pass each other on the water (*Excidio Trojae Historia*, 9). In the lost *Cypria*, Paris was the guest of Menelaus for several days before the latter departed for Crete (Proclus, *Chrestomathy*, I).

24. Sir Dares is presumably the author, who "saw that war, without fail / And did write that same battle" (ll. 15-16). The original Dares was a Trojan (see note 1), which may explain why MS. Harl. 525 substitutes him for Ulysses.

25. This description of Menelaus as having red hair and a moderate stature comes directly from Dares (*Excidio Trojae Historia*, 13).

26. The "Catalogue of Ships" in the *Seege of Troye* would require a long digression to fully compare and contrast with its classical predecessors, so I have devoted **Appendix III** to this end. One immediate difference is the poet only naming one leader per contingent, when many of the Homeric ships had multiple commanders of equal authority. The Argives under Diomedes are conspicuously absent—the son of Tydeus does not appear in the *Seege* at all, which is unusual given his prominence in the mythology. Achilles is also missing, as he has not yet been fetched from the court of King Lycomedes.

27. This is a remnant of Dares Phrygius combining the Salaminian contingent under Telamonian Ajax and Teucer with the Eleans under Amphimachus, Thalpius, Diores and Polyxenus (see **Appendix III**).

28. Here the brothers Podarces and Protesilaus lead separate contingents. Dares Phrygius places them together (*Excidio Trojae Historia*, 14); in the *Iliad* Podarces is described as his elder brother's subordinate, having assumed command of the Phylacians when Protesilaus was slain (II.695-710).

29. These quantities do not actually add up to 1,255 (see **Appendix III**).

30. MSS. Harl. 525 and Egerton 2862 have Ulysses visit the shrine of Apollo instead of Dares (see note 24). In Dares Phrygius, Agamemnon sends Achilles and Patroclus (*Excidio Trojae Historia*, 15).

31. In Dares Phrygius, Agamemnon is chosen as commander-in-chief by the Greeks (*Excidio Trojae Historia*, 11).

32. Here there is no mention of any attempt by the Trojans to prevent the Greek ships from landing; in Dares Phrygius (and also the lost *Cypria*) the Trojans fiercely defend their shores until they are driven back by Achilles (*Excidio Trojae Historia*, 19; Proclus, *Chrestomathy*, I).

33. Protesilaus was the first Greek to die at Troy (Apollodorus, *Bibliotheca*, E.3.30); in Dares and its medieval offshoots this detail is lost, although he is generally the first "named" character to be slain (*Excidio Trojae Historia*, 19). Here the war has been raging for four years before his death. Note how in MS. Lincoln's Inn 150 he is merely unhorsed—only MS. Harl. 525 actually describes his death.

34. In Book II of Homer's *Iliad*, Patroclus is slain commanding the Myrmidons in Achilles' absence, the latter refusing to fight on account of Agamemnon's appropriation of Briseis. In Dares (*Excidio Trojae Historia*, 19), Achilles does not withdraw from battle until after the death of Hector, so he is apparently on the field when Patroclus dies (although it is Meriones who rescues his body). The *Seege of Troye* combines the narratives of Dares Phrygius with the

Rawlinson Excidium Troiae, which places Achilles on Skyros at the beginning of the war, and as a result Patroclus dies before the son of Peleus even arrives at Troy.

35. This appears to be a mangled version of the duel between Menelaus and Paris in *Iliad* III. Paris is swiftly defeated, but is cloaked in a mist and spirited from the field by the goddess Aphrodite before Menelaus can slay him. In the aftermath, Pandarus—at the urging of Athena—looses an arrow at Menelaus and wounds him in the torso.

36. The detail of the siege beginning without Achilles comes from the *Rawlinson Excidium Troiae*, in which he is not summoned from Lycomedes' court until after the Greek armies have landed at Troy.

37. Here Peleus is conflated with the centaur Chiron, who is said to have tutored the young Achilles (Apollodorus, *Bibliotheca*, III.13.6).

38. Lycomedes' court was at Skyros (Proclus, *Chrestomathy*, I). Exactly where "the land of Parchy" ("Parpachy" in Harl. 525) is supposed to represent is unclear, but Wager and Barnicle interpret it as Sparta.

39. The episode of Achilles disguised as a woman at the court of King Lycomedes comes from the *Rawlinson Excidium Troiae*. Along with the youth of Paris among the shepherds, its origin was a source of confusion for early scholars, as it does not appear in Dares or Dictys (see note 13). The story is told more fully in the *Achilleid*—an unfinished epic poem by the first-century Roman poet Statius.

40. This line seems to be extraneous, forming the poem's only tristich. It is not present in the Egerton and Arundel manuscripts.

41. In Harl. 525 Achilles causes the sparks to fly from Hector's helm.

42. MS. Harl. 525 is unique in that Hector actually manages to wound Achilles, despite his skin supposedly being "hard as baleen".

43. Note how the helm is simply lying on the ground in the Lincoln's Inn text, with no mention made of its owner. Harl. 525 is much closer to Dares Phrygius (*Excidio Trojae Historia*, 24), in which Hector strips the armour from the fallen Polypoetes ("Syr Annys" in the Middle English text).

44. This line is missing from the Lincoln's Inn version—I have borrowed it from MS. Arundel XXII to complete the couplet.

45. This is Dares Phrygius' version of Achilles' withdrawal from battle, which is on account of Polyxena instead of Briseis (*Excidio Troiae Historia*, 27-30). Achilles' fascination with the Trojan princess is a later development in the mythology (Homer does not mention her at all), but the connection between the two characters goes back to the lost *Iliu Persis*, in which Polyxena was sacrificed at Achilles' tomb (Proclus, *Chrestomathy*, II); this event formed

the subject of Euripides' *Hecuba*. Polyxena is also present at Achilles' slaying of Troilus in early depictions of the event (Attic black figure kylix, c. 570-565 BC, Louvre CA6113; Laconian black-figured dinos, c. 560-540 BC, Louvre E662), which may reflect the story once contained in the lost *Cypria*.

46. This episode is drawn from the burning of the Greek ships in Book XV of Homer's *Iliad*, although here—as per Dares Phrygius—Troilus takes the place of his brother Hector (*Excidio Trojae Historia*, 28).

47. In early literature and various surviving depictions of the incident, Troilus was practically a child when he was slain by Achilles in an ambush (Horace, *Odes*, II.9.13-16). Dares made him older and a capable warrior, holding his own in the ranks with his brothers; from this (via Benoît's *Roman de Troie*) came the medieval conception of Troilus as a "second Hector".

48. In Dares the "young knight" was Antilochus, son of Nestor (*Excidio Trojae Historia*, 34).

49. This is essentially Dares' version of the death of Achilles, although the ambush in the *Excidio* consists of only a handful of men, and Achilles' corpse is returned to the Greeks at the urging of Helenus (*Excidio Trojae Historia*, 34). In the lost *Aethiopis* Achilles, having driven the Trojans to the very gates of the city, was slain by Paris with an arrow guided by Apollo (Proclus, *Chrestomathy*, II).

50. These three lines form a tristich in MS. Harl. 525.

51. In Harl. 525, "And thus died that doughty knight" is the first line of the couplet.

52. In Quintus Smyrnaeus' *Posthomerica*, Paris is mortally wounded by Philoctetes with an arrow. He goes to Mount Ida to be healed by the nymph Oenone—the wife he deserted for Helen—but she refuses, and he dies on the mountain. After his death, the grief-stricken Oenone throws herself onto his funeral pyre (*Posthomerica*, X.272-519).

53. This version of Ajax' death comes from Dares (*Excidio Trojae Historia*, 35). The son of Telamon traditionally committed suicide after losing the contest for Achilles' arms, having come to his senses after a bout of madness in which he slaughtered the Greeks' cattle, mistaking them for those who had betrayed him by awarding the arms to Ulysses (Sophocles, *Ajax*; Apollodorus, *Bibliotheca*, E.5.6-7; Proclus, *Chrestomathy*, II).

54. The Lincoln's Inn manuscript jumps from the eight battle to the tenth. MSS. Egerton 2862 and Arundel XXII each include a couplet counting the death of Achilles as a battle, which seems to have been accidentally omitted by the Lincoln's Inn scribe.

55. The treason of Antenor and Aeneas was not a feature of the Homeric or Cyclic tradition of the fall of Troy, but appears in Dictys and Dares (*Ephemeris Belli Trojani*, IV.22; *Excidio Trojae Historia*, 39), and was accepted as the "canonical" version by medieval readers. The story must be relatively early, as it was known to the 4th century BC historian Menecrates of Xanthus, although his account of the betrayal implicated Aeneas only (Dionysius of Halicarnassus, *Roman Antiquities*, I.48.3).

56. The poet of the *Seege of Troye* follows Dares Phrygius in omitting the famous "Trojan Horse", with the traitors Antenor and Aeneas opening the gates for the Greeks. Dares mentions a carved horse's head above the Scaean Gate—opened by the traitors—as a nod to the original myth (*Excidio Trojae Historia*, 40).

57. In the lost *Little Iliad*, Pyrrhus was fetched from the court of King Lycomedes by Ulysses after the death of Achilles (Proclus, *Chrestomathy*, II). With no mention of him up to this point, one might assume that in this version he journeyed to Troy with his father.

58. The *Seege of Troye* here presents Neoptolemus as simply murdering Polyxena; she was traditionally offered as a sacrifice to appease the ghost of Achilles (Proclus, *Chrestomathy*, II; Euripides, *Hecuba*).

59. As with Dares Phrygius' *Excidio Trojae Historia*, the *Seege of Troye* ends without any mention of the disasters that befell the Greeks in the war's aftermath (as described in Aeschylus' *Oresteia* trilogy, the lost epic *Nostoi*, and Homer's *Odyssey*).

THE RAWLINSON PROSE SIEGE OF TROY

1. Refers to Guido delle Collone's *Historia Destructionis Troiae*, of which Lydgate's *Troy Book* is a verse translation. This led earlier scholars to suppose the text to be a redaction of Guido, as Lydgate is nowhere mentioned.

2. The name of Jason's mother varies between sources. In the *Argonautica* she is Alcimede (I.45-8), daughter of Phylacus (founder of Phylace, and grandfather of Protesilaus and Podarces); other authors made her Polymede (Apollodorus, *Bibliotheca*, I.9.16; Hesiod, *Catalogue of Women*, Fragment 13), the daughter of Autolycus (and thus the sister of Anticlea, the mother of Ulysses). At least five other possible candidates are recorded, but here Medea is a clear error. The author of the *Rawl.*—probably confused by an early reference to Medea's rejuvenation of Aeson in *Troy Book* (I.131-145)—incorrectly assumes her to be a separate character from the daughter of King Aeëtes who

wedded Jason. According to Ovid, Aeson's youth was restored as a favour to Jason upon their return from Colchis (*Metamorphoses*, VII.159-296).

3. See *Seege of Troye* note 4.

4. "Jaconites" comes from Benoît's *Roman de Troie* (l. 1163). There was no such city in historical Colchis.

5. Medea was not traditionally the sole heir of Aeëtes. In most versions of the Golden Fleece myth Aeëtes had a son, Absyrtus, who was murdered by either Jason or Medea during their flight from Colchis (Apollodorus, *Bibliotheca*, I.9.23-24).

6. This story forms the subject of Euripides' *Medea.*

7. The Thessalian King Pelias was not traditionally present at the destruction of Laomedon's Troy. In medieval versions, beginning with Benoît's *Roman de Troie*, he is conflated with Peleus (ll. 145-160)—the father of Achilles and brother of Telamon—who was both an Argonaut and (in at least one version of the story) a companion of Hercules on his expedition to Troy (Apollodorus, *Bibliotheca*, I.9.16; Dares Phrygius, *Excidio Trojae Historia*, 3).

8. The author of the *Rawl.* here repeats Lydgate's error in making Telamon the King of Messina (*Troy Book,* I.3823-3832). The mistake only appears once in *Troy Book*, with Telamon correctly named as King of Salamis in all other instances.

9. Helen was the stepdaughter of King Tyndareus of Sparta, whose wife Leda was impregnated by Jupiter (Apollodorus, *Bibliotheca*, III.10.7). The error comes from the *Historia Destructionis Troiae* of Guido delle Collone, who associated her with the city of Tyndaris in his native Sicily (IV.10-17).

10. In Benoît's *Roman de Troie* the mouth of the Simoeis River becomes "the haven of Simoënta" (l.983). Tenedos is an island in the Aegean southwest of Troy—according to the lost *Little Iliad*, this was where the Greeks hid their fleet when they pretended to abandon the siege (Proclus, *Chrestomathy*, II).

11. The wording here implies that Laomedon was slain by Jason, when he was in fact slain by Hercules (John Lydgate, *Troy Book*, I.4299-4310).

12. See *Seege of Troye* note 9.

13. The name Ilion/Ilium traditionally refers to the city itself; the name of Priam's citadel was Pergamum or Pergamos (Homer, *Iliad*, IV.446 ff).

14. Ganymede was typically said to be the son of Tros, the first King of Troy, and thus the great-uncle of Priam (Homer, *Iliad*, XX.232).

15. Note that Paris' judgement of the goddesses is omitted in this version.

16. In *Troy Book* Menelaus is in Pylos visiting Nestor (II.4276-7). According to Apollodorus he went to Crete for the funeral of his maternal grandfather Catreus, the son of King Minos (*Bibliotheca*, E.3.3).

17. The temple on Cythera was to Venus—not Diana. Interestingly, Dares Phrygius mentions Paris sacrificing to Diana upon his arrival but Lydgate does not (*Excidio Trojae Historia*, 9-10). N. E. Griffin believed this was evidence that the account is partly based on Dares (1907, p. 166), but it seems just as likely to be a case of the author getting his goddesses mixed up.

18. The author of the *Rawl.* omits Castor and Pollux' ill-fated expedition to recover their sister, which ends with their deaths in a shipwreck (*Troy Book*, II.4448-4483). This version comes from Dares Phrygius (*Excidio Trojae Historia*, 11); in the mythological tradition Castor—the mortal son of Tyndareus—was slain attempting to steal the cattle of his cousins Idas and Lynceus. His brother Pollux, who was the son of Jupiter, begged his father to allow him to share his immortality with Castor, and they became the constellation Gemini (Apollodorus, *Bibliotheca*, III.11.12). The *Seege of Troye* also contains no mention of their fate.

19. As with the Catalogue of Ships in the *Seege of Troye* (see *Seege of Troye* note 26), I have devoted **Appendix III** to a detailed comparison between this list of the Greek leaders and its literary forebears from Homer to Lydgate. This version contains a number of variations from *Troy Book*'s Catalogue, and erroneously lists a number of Trojan allies among the Greeks (all of those after Treorius of Beysa are Trojan).

20. Here the sons of Aesculapius are duplicated; this comes from the author combining Lydgate's list of character portraits (*Troy Book* II.4509-5054) with his Catalogue of Ships (*Troy Book* II.5105-5198), and not identifying where they overlap (see **Appendix III**).

21. See note 10.

22. In *Troy Book* Hector slays Patroclus (III.772-791), Nireus (III.1744-1756) and Meriones during this battle (III.1889-1904).

23. In *Troy Book* Hector slays the Boeotian brothers Arcesilaus and Prothoenor during this battle (III.2594-2632). Deiphobus is not slain until after the death of Hector, when he his mortally wounded by Palamedes—who is himself slain by Paris as his brother lays dying (IV.1567-1586). In the lost *Iliu Persis*, Deiphobus—having married Helen after the death of Paris—was killed by Menelaus during the sack of Troy (Proclus, *Chrestomathy*, II).

24. In Lydgate's *Troy Book* Calchas joins the Greeks much earlier, meeting Achilles at the Temple of Apollo before the invasion (II.6013-6023). The incident does not appear in the *Rawl.*, but a version appears in the *Seege of Troye* (ll. 935-968), with "Sir Dares" taking the place of Achilles.

25. In *Troy Book* Hector slays Orcomeneus, Epistrophus, Schedius, Elephenor, Diores and Polyxenus during this battle (III.3338-3517).

26. In *Troy Book* Antenor is traded for the Aetolian King Thoas, with Calchas persuading the Greeks to demand his daughter as part of the bargain (III.4231-2). This is the only mention of Cressida in the *Rawl.*—her famous "love triangle" with Troilus and Diomedes (described by Chaucer and Shakespeare) is omitted entirely. She is also absent from the *Seege of Troye*.

27. Pirus was a Thracian, and an ally of the Trojans (see note 19). In Lydgate's *Troy Book* the first Greek to be slain by Hector upon his return to battle is Eurypylus (III.5250-3).

28. In Dares, Hector is stripping the armour of Polypoetes when he is taken unawares by Achilles (*Excidio Trojae Historia*, 24). Benoît's *Roman de Troie* adds a nameless Greek king after Polypoetes (ll.16215-16221), and Lydgate's *Troy Book* follows this (III.5332-5353). Palamedes is slain by Paris after Hector's death, having killed Sarpedon and mortally wounded Deiphobus (*Troy Book*, III.1317-1377). According to classical sources Palamedes was either murdered by Ulysses and Diomedes (Proclus, *Chrestomathy*, I; Dictys Cretensis, *Ephemeris Belli Trojani*, II.15), or framed by Ulysses as a traitor and stoned to death by the Greeks (Hyginus, *Fabulae*, 105; Apollodorus, *Bibliotheca*, E.3.8).

29. Lydgate lists eighteen kings slain by Hector: Protesilaus, Patroclus, Meriones (of Crete), Arcesilaus, Prothoenor, Elephenor, Phidippus, Epistrophus, Antiphus, Merion (a kinsman of Achilles), Schedius, Diores, Polyxenus, Polypoetes, Leonteus, Boëtes, Iphinous, and Nireus. He does not count Eurypylus—the King of Thessaly in Homer, reduced to a mere duke in the medieval tradition (IV.26-48).

30. In *Troy Book* it is Menelaus who objects to the treaty, as there is no mention of Paris relinquishing Helen (IV.1915-1950).

31. See *Seege of Troye* note 45.

32. In Lydgate's *Troy Book* Troilus slays a thousand knights on his rampage, but no "named" characters (IV.2040-2).

33. In the *Roman de Troie*, Benoît has Troilus dragged behind Achilles' horse in Hector's stead (ll.21397-21450); this was possibly influenced by Dictys' account of the death of Hector, as there is no such incident in Dares (*Ephemeris Belli Trojani*, III.15). The mutilation of Troilus' corpse may be an embellishment by Benoît, although there was a tradition of Achilles disfiguring the body, appearing in a lost play by Sophocles (Sophocles, *Troilus*, Fragment 623).

34. See *Seege of Troye* note 49.

35. The author of the *Rawl.* here omits the arrival of Neoptolemus from Skyros and his defeat of Penthesilea, Queen of the Amazons. In the lost *Aethi-*

opis Penthesilea was slain by Achilles (Proclus, *Chrestomathy*, II), but the medieval tradition (following Dares) places her arrival after the death of Paris (Dares Phrygius, *Excidio Trojae Historia*, 36).

36. See *Seege of Troye* note 55.

37. The Homeric Trojan Horse was devised by Ulysses and built by Epeius. It was traditionally made of wood—not brass (Quintus Smyrnaeus, *Posthomerica*, XII.21-85).

38. Medieval accounts dramatically upscale the Trojan Horse to a behemoth capable of holding a thousand warriors. The classical version was built of wood, and held between thirty (Quintus Smyrnaeus, *Posthomerica*, XII.337-359) and fifty Greek warriors (Apollodorus, *Bibliotheca*, E.5.14).

39. This is the only mention of Neoptolemus in the *Rawl.*, aside from his bizarre appearance in the list of Greek leaders. This gives the mistaken impression that he was at the siege from the beginning.

40. In Lydgate's *Troy Book*, Aeneas is exiled from Troy as a punishment for attempting to hide Polyxena from the Greeks. After the Greeks have departed he returns to the city and lays an ambush for Antenor (who revealed her location), but is prevented from slaying him by the remaining Trojans (V.358-520).

APPENDIX I.

A Glossary of Names

Throughout my translation I have reverted to the Latin or Latinised Greek spellings of all those names which derive from the Classical/mythological canon. I here list the names of all characters appearing in the *Seege of Troy* and the *Rawlinson Prose Siege of Troy* along with the original Middle English spelling.

Refer to **Appendix III** for an in-depth analysis of the "Catalogue of Ships" portions of the *Seege of Troy* and the *Rawlinson Prose Siege of Troy*.

HL: *Seege of Troye*, Harleian MS. 525
LI: *Seege of Troye*, Lincoln's Inn MS. 150
RW: The *Rawlinson Prose Siege of Troy*

Achilles, *Acheldes,*[HL] *Achelles,*[HL] *Achilles,*[ALL] *Achyl(l)es,*[HL] leader of the Myrmidons; son of **Peleus** and **Thetis**
Aeëtes, *Sithes,*[RW] King of Colchis; father of **Medea**
Aeneas, *Eneas,*[ALL] *Enneas,*[HL] Trojan hero of the *Aeneid*
Aeson, *Eson,*[RW] father of **Jason**

Agamemnon, *Agaman,*[LI] *Agamanoun,*[HL] *Agamenon,*[RW] *Agamenoun,*[HL] *Agamon,*[LI] *Agamynon,*[HL] King of Mycenae; brother of **Menelaus**

Agapenor, *Carpenor,*[RW] *Sarpenor,*[LI] King of Arcadia; Greek ally

Ajax,[i] *Aiax,*[HL, LI] *Talamon,*[HL] *Telamus,*[RW] *Tolemew,*[HL] Salaminean leader; son of **Telamon**

Ajax,[ii] *Arax,*[RW] *Castor of Locry,*[LI] Locrian leader; son of **Oileus**

Alexander (Paris), *Alisaunder,*[HL, LI] *Alysaunder,*[HL, LI] son of **Priam**

Antenor, *Antenor,*[RW] *Antynor,*[LI] *Ent(e)mor(e),*[HL] Trojan elder and counsellor

Antiphus,[i] *Ancipe,*[LI] *Amphimachus,*[RW] Calydnian leader; brother of **Phidippus**; Greek ally

Antiphus,[ii] *Antiphis,*[RW] Elean leader; Greek ally

Antiphus,[iii] *Ampheus,*[RW] Maeonian leader; Trojan ally (listed among the Greeks in the *Rawlinson Prose Siege of Troy*)

Arcesilaus, *Archelay,*[LI] *Archeley,*[HL] Boeotian leader; Greek ally

Archilochus, *Archiligus,*[RW] Thracian leader; Trojan ally (listed among the Greeks in the *Rawlinson Prose Siege of Troy*)

Ascalaphus, *Askelop,*[HL] *Astolope,*[LI] King of Orchomenus; Greek ally

Calchas, *Calcas,*[RW] priest of Apollo, father of **Cressida**

Cassandra, *Cassandra,*[RW] daughter of **Priam**

Castor, *Castor,*[ALL] twin brother of **Pollux,** brother of **Helen**

Cressida, *Criseide,*[RW] daughter of **Calchas** (derives from the Briseis of the *Iliad*)

Creusa, *Granchia,*[RW] wife of **Aeneas**

Dares, *Dares,*[LI] *Darras,*[HL] Trojan priest of Vulcan; supposed author of the *Excidio Trojae Historia* (becomes a Greek in the Lincoln's Inn *Seege of Troye*)

Deidamia, *Dyademades,*[HL] *-medes,*[HL] *Tyamedes,*[LI] daughter of **Lycomedes**; mother of **Neoptolemus**

Deiphobus, *Deyphebus,*[RW] son of **Priam**

Diomedes, *Diomede,*[RW] *Dyomede,*[RW] King of Argos

Diores, *Eros,*[RW] Elean leader; Greek ally

Epistrophus,[i] *Etrop,*[LI] *Epistrophis,*[RW] Phocian leader; Greek ally

Epistrophus,[ii] *Epistrophus,*[RW] Halizone leader; Trojan ally (listed among the Greeks in the *Rawlinson Prose Siege of Troy*)

Eumelus, *Ampedy*[LI] Pheraean leader; Greek ally

Euryalus, *Eriale,*[RW] companion of **Diomedes**

Eurypylus, *Ermupil,*[LI] King of Thessaly, Greek ally

Ganymede, *Gamenede,*[RW] Trojan prince (Lydgate and the *Rawlinson Prose Siege of Troy* author make him the son of **Priam**; he was traditionally the son of Tros, the first King of Troy)

Guneus, *Sennes,*[HL] *Ywayn,*[LI] leader of the Aenianes and Perrhaebians; Greek ally

Hector, *Ectour,*[HL] *Ector,*[HL, LI] *Etour,*[HL] son of **Priam**

Hecuba, *Ecuba,*[LI & RW] *Ekeuba,*[HL] Queen of Troy; wife of **Priam**

Helen, *Elayne,*[LI] *Elen,*[HL] *Elyn,*[HL & RW] *Elyne,*[HL] Queen of Sparta; lover of **Paris**

Helenus, *Elacyus,*[RW] son of **Priam**

Hercules, *Ercules,*[ALL] Greek hero

Hesione, *Exeona,*[RW] *Isyon,*[HL] *Vsian,*[LI] *Vsion,*[LI] *Ysyon,*[HL] daughter of **Laomedon**; sister of **Priam**

Idomeneus, *Edomeyne,*[LI] King of Crete

Jason, *Jason,*[ALL] *Jasonne,*[HL] *Jasoun,*[LI] leader of the Argonauts; son of **Aeson**

Laomedon, *Lamadan,*[HL] *-tan,*[HL] *Lamedon,*[RW] *Leomadan,*[LI] *Limadan,*[HL] *Lymadan,*[HL] *-don(e),*[HL] *-down,*[HL] King of Troy; father of **Priam** and **Hesione**

Lycomedes, *Likamedes,*[HL] *Lycamedes,*[LI] *Lykamedes,*[HL] *-mydes,*[LI] King of Scyros; father of **Deidamia**

Machaon, *Makary,*[RW] *Mathaon,*[RW] son of Aesculapius; brother of **Podalirius**; Greek ally

Medea, *Medea,*[RW] Princess of Colchis; daughter of **Aeëtes**

Menelaus, *Melany,*[RW] *Menaly,*[HL] *Menelaus,*[RW] *-lay,*[RW] *Menolay,*[HL, LI] *Monal(a)y,*[HL] *Monayl,*[HL] *Mon-el(a)y,*[HL] King of Sparta; husband of **Helen**

Menestheus, *Monastew,*[HL] *Monstow,*[LI] King of Athens; Greek ally

Mopsus, *Cariac,*[RW] Colophonian leader; Trojan ally (listed among the Greeks in the *Rawlinson Prose Siege of Troy*)

Neoptolemus (Pyrrhus), *Neptalamus,*[HL] *Neptolomys,*[RW] son of **Achilles** and **Deidamia**

Nestor, *Duke Philon,*[RW] *Hectour,*[HL] *Nesto(u)r,*[HL, LI] *Necto(u)r, Nastor,*[HL] King of Pylos; Greek ally

Oileus, *Cylyus,*[RW] Greek hero; father of **Ajax**[ii]

Palamedes, *Pallamydes,*[RW] *Palmydes,*[HL, LI] *Namply of Palamyde,*[LI] Euboean leader; son of Nauplius

Paris, *Paris,*[HL] *Parys,*[HL & RW] *Paryse,*[HL, LI] *Parysse,*[HL] son of **Priam**; lover of **Helen**

Patroclus, *Padradod(e),*[HL] *Parpadode,*[HL] *Patroclus,*[RW] *Patrode,*[LI] *Potroclus,*[RW] *Tendalus,*[RW] companion of **Achilles**

Pelias, *Pelles,*[HL] *Pelleus,*[RW] *Pelyas,*[LI] *Pilleus,*[RW] *Pyllios,*[RW] King of Iolcus; uncle of **Jason** (see **Peleus**)

Peleus, *Pelles,*[HL] *Pyles,*[LI] King of Phthia; father of **Achilles** (The author of the *Rawlinson Prose Siege of Troy*, following Lydgate, does not distinguish between **Pcleus** and **Pelias**)

Perses, *Porces,*[RW] Ethiopian leader; Trojan ally (listed among the Greeks in the *Rawlinson Prose Siege of Troy*)

Phidippus, *Pollibete,*[RW] Calydnian leader; brother of **Antiphus**[i]; Greek ally

Philoctetes, *Philete,*[LI] *Pilotes,*[RW] *Polliphebus,*[RW] companion of **Hercules**; Greek ally

Phorcys, *Forcunus,*[RW] Phrygian leader; Trojan ally (listed among the Greeks in the *Rawlinson Prose Siege of Troy*)

Pirus, *Philex,*[RW] Thracian leader; Trojan ally (listed among the Greeks in the *Rawlinson Prose Siege of Troy*)

Podalirius, *Polinestor,*[LI] *Pollidrus,*[RW] *Pollydamas,*[RW] son of Aesculapius, brother of **Machaon**; Greek ally

Podarces, *Podam,*[LI] *Podane,*[HL] brother of **Protesilaus**; Greek ally

Pollux, *Pollex,*[HL, LI] *Pollux,*[RW] twin brother of **Castor**, brother of **Helen**

Polydorus, *Palliodorus,*[RW] son of **Priam**

Polypoetes, *An(n)ys,*[HL] *Polipete,*[LI] Lapith leader; son of Pirithous; Greek ally

Polyxena, *Pollicene,*[RW] *Polixene,*[RW] *Pollexene,*[HL] *Polluxene,*[LI] daughter of **Priam**

Polyxenus, *Pollex,*[HL] Elean leader; Greek ally

Priam(us), *Priamus,*[ALL] *Pryamus,*[HL] King of Troy, son of **Laomedon**

Protesilaus, *Portislay,*[HL, LI] *Portuflay,*[HL] *Protheselay,*[RW] *Prothesilaus,*[RW] King of Phylace; brother of **Podarces**; Greek ally

Prothous, *Prestolay,*[LI] Magnesian leader; Greek ally

Pylaemenes, *Philanyme,*[RW] King of Paphlagonia; Trojan ally (listed among the Greeks in the *Rawlinson Prose Siege of Troy*)

Pyrrhus (Neoptolemus), *Pirrus,*[LI] son of **Achilles** and **Deidamia**

Rhesus, *Terenes,*[RW] King of Thrace; Trojan ally (listed among the Greeks in the *Rawlinson Prose Siege of Troy*)

Sigamon, *Sygamon,*[RW] Ethiopian leader, brother of Memnon (a non-Cyclic character from Benoît's *Roman de Troie*, listed among the Greeks in the *Rawlinson Prose Siege of Troy*)

Telamon, *T(h)alamon,*[ALL] *Tallamo,*[HL] father of **Ajax**[i]; King of Salamis

Thetis, *Tetes,*[LI] *Tytes,*[HL] mother of **Achilles**; wife of **Peleus**

Thoas, *Tholas,*[LI] Aetolian leader; Greek ally

Tlepolemus, *Theofele,*[LI] King of Rhodes; son of **Hercules**

Treorius, *Trearius,*[RW] King of Beysa; Greek ally (a non-Cyclic character, derived from "Creneus of Pyle" who appears in some medieval copies of Dares Phrygius' *Excidio Trojae Historia*)

Troilus, *Troell,*[HL] *Troilus,*[RW] *Troyel(l),*[HL] *Troyl(l)e,*[LI] *Troylus,*[RW] son of **Priam**

Ulysses, *Elux(i)es,*[HL] *Euluxes,*[HL] *Ulex,*[LI] *Vlixes,*[RW] King of Ithaca; hero of the *Odyssey*

APPENDIX II.

A Glossary of Middle English, Archaic & Obscure Words

againward, *adv.,* back again; in return
aketon, *n.,* a padded jacket worn under mail
arbalest, *n.,* a crossbow
awreak, *v.,* avenge
bale, *n.,* torment; suffering
bascinet, *n.,* a type of medieval helmet
bestood, *v.,* at the ready; nearby
blive, *adj.,* quickly
bote, *n.,* benefit
cader, *n.,* a cradle
caitiff, *n.,* a wretch
countermure, *n.,* a secondary wall in a fortification, behind the first
couth, *v.,* could
crouth, *n.,* a type of stringed instrument
dare, *v.,* to lie motionless
dere, *n.,* hurt; harm
dight, *adj.,* equipped; furnished
dight, *v.,* equip; furnish
disport, *v.,* to play or relax
disour, *n.,* a storyteller
donjon, *n.,* the main tower or keep of a castle
faitour, *n,* a deceiver or imposter
fane, *n.,* a banner
ferly, *n,* surprise; wonder

fode, *n.,* a youth, or a young warrior
forsooth, *adv.,* for truth; indeed
forthy, *adv.,* therefore
freely, *adj.,* free; noble
gambeson, *n.,* a padded jacket
gang, *v.,* go; proceed
gin, *n.,* trickery; guile
graith, *v.,* to make ready
halfendeal, *adv.,* half
hauberk, *n.,* a coat of mail
hende (i), *adj.,* courteous; gentle
hende (ii), *adj.,* ready; prompt
hie, *n. or v.,* haste
hight, *adj.,* named; called
hying, *n.,* hastening
iwis., *adv.,* certainly; indeed
leman, *n.,* a lover or sweetheart
let, *v.,* to hinder; delay
lite, *adj.,* little
lorn, *adj.,* lost
losenger, *n.,* a deceiver; a flatterer
machicolation, *n.,* an overhanging parapet, through which stones can be dropped or arrows shot onto besiegers
main, *n.,* a lord's retinue or household
mammet, *n.,* an idol
mammetry, *n.,* idol worship
maugre, *prep.,* despite
meed, *n.,* reward or merit
mickle, *adj.,* much; great
mold, *n.,* ground; the surface of the earth
moot, *v.,* to debate
mote, *v.,* might or may ("mote I thee" = might I thrive)
naker, *n.,* a type of drum
nigromancy, *n.,* black magic

nome, *v.,* take or took
nonce, *n.,* the now; the time being
peradventure, *adv.,* perchance; perhaps
peridot, *n.,* an olive-green gemstone
pery, *n.,* precious stones
planchette, *n.,* a small plank (French)
plenar, *adv.,* full; complete
polke, *n.,* a puddle or pool
porture, *n.,* deportment
poustie, *n.,* power
prow, *n.,* benefit; advantage
psalterer, *n.,* one who plays on a psaltery (a stringed instrument)
pyment, *n.,* a type of mead
rede, *n.,* advice; instruction
rede, *v.,* to advise; help
rode, *n.,* complexion
ruth, *n.,* pity
saw, *n.,* saying; speech
sendal, *n.,* a type of light silk
scathe, *n.,* harm; misfortune
shend, *v.,* to shame or destroy
somedeal, *adv.,* somewhat; partly
sooth, *n.,* truth; reality
springal, *n.,* a catapult
stound (i), *n.,* a period of time; a moment
stound (ii), *n.,* a shock or a blow
stour, *n.,* a conflict
swain, *n.,* squire
swithe (i), *adv.,* quickly
swithe (ii), *adv.,* very; exceedingly
tabor, *n.,* a type of drum
tharms, *n.,* entrails; intestines
tide, *n.,* time
unmeet, *adj.,* improper

unride, *adj.,* cruel; savage
verrament, *adv.,* verily; indeed
victualled, *adj.,* equipped
weed(s), *n.,* clothing
ween, *n.,* doubt
wellaway, *interj.,* a cry of sadness; alas
wend, *v.,* to turn or make one's way
wight (i), *adj.,* strong; mighty
wight (ii), *n.,* a person or living creature
wist, *v.,* past tense of **wit**
wit, *v.,* to know; understand
wode, *adj.,* mad, enraged
wot, *v.,* to know; understand
wreak, *v.,* to take revenge
yode, *v.,* to go or walk

APPENDIX III.

The "Catalogue of Ships" from Homer to the Middle Ages

THE "Catalogue of Ships" in the *Seege of Troye* and the list of Greek leaders in the *Rawlinson Prose Siege of Troy* have a complex lineage spanning multiple literary works. They share a common ancestor in the *Excidio Trojae Historia* of Dares Phrygius (which ultimately derives from Book II of Homer's *Iliad*), but where the *Seege of Troye's* connection to Dares is more or less direct, the *Rawlinson Prose Siege of Troy* is separated by three generations. Their lines of descent may be illustrated thus:

Homer's *Iliad*
|
Dares Phrygius' *Excidio Trojae Historia*
| |
The Seege of Troye Benoît's *Roman de Troie*
|
Guido's *Historia Destructionis Troiae*
|
John Lydgate's *Troy Book*
|
The *Rawlinson Prose Siege of Troy*

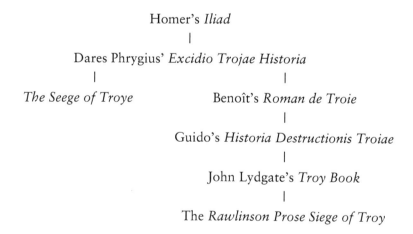

On the following pages I present the "Catalogue of Ships" portions of the above works in a series of tables, tracing their development from author to author. The tables have been sequenced according to Dares Phrygius rather than Homer, as the catalogues of Benoît, Guido and Lydgate (and to a small degree the *Seege of Troye*) all follow the pattern of the *Excidio Trojae Historia*. I have made one exception, setting Dares' Elean contingent of Antiphus and Amphimachus (usually placed between Eurypylus and Polypoetes) opposite Homer's Elean contingent of Amphimachus, Diores, Thalpius and Polyxenus—in Dares, the latter four travel with Telamonian Ajax and Teucer.

The catalogue of Dares Phrygius seems to be closely modelled on Homer's with a few changes—along with the additional Elean leaders, Nireus of Syme somehow gains an extra fifty ships(!), and the contingents led by Elephenor and Meges disappear.* Dares also restricts himself to naming one settlement per contingent—in contrast with Homer's practice of listing of individual cities, citadels, towns, islands, down to the smallest village.† Due to limited space, I give only the primary settlements in the table from the *Iliad*.

Dares' catalogue is still identifiable in the *Seege of Troye*, albeit with many of the names Anglicised beyond recognition. The *Seege* is unique in that it only lists one leader per navy. Achilles is absent, as he does not enter the war until after the Greeks besiege Troy, but Diomedes is a glaring omission, and does not feature in the poem at all. "Sir Dares"—presumably representing the fictional author of the *Excidio Trojae Historia*—appears as a lord of "Parchy" (Sparta?), although in the Harleian MS. his place is occupied by "Sir Eluxes" (Ulysses).

Benoît de Sainte-Maure's catalogue is relatively unchanged from Dares. Notable deviations are an extra fifty ships for Ulysses, and the addition of "Crenos de Pisa"—an obscure character who appears in late copies of Dares' *Excidio* as "Creneus of Pylos". Through Benoît

* Elephenor is still named by Dares as one of the leaders slain by Hector, but Meges has completely vanished, and is absent from the medieval tradition

† "And they that held Mycenae, the well-built citadel, and wealthy Corinth, and well-built Cleonae, and dwelt in Orneiae and lovely Araethyrea and Sicyon...and they that held Hyperesia and steep Gonoessa and Pellene, and that dwelt about Aegium and throughout all Aegialus, and about broad Helice—of these was the son of Atreus, lord Agamemnon, captain..." *Iliad*, II.569-579

this apparent scribal error becomes a permanent fixture of the medieval catalogue. Guido delle Collone adds and subtracts a few ships here and there, also dropping Menestheus of Athens despite the character's relative prominence elsewhere in the narrative.

By the time we reach John Lydgate's *Troy Book* it is interesting to note that nine of the original Homeric contingents still contain the same number of ships. Lydgate follows Guido closely, but combines the navies of Thoas and the "King of Daymes" (Nireus), and omits Eurypylus (the latter still appears in the poem as "Curibulus").

At first glance, the catalogue found in the *Rawlinson Prose Siege of Troy* appears to be Lydgate's reduced to a bare list of names, but its true origins are rather more complex. In her 1951 thesis published in the journal *Speculum*,* C. R. B. Combellack identified the catalogue as the composite of four different passages within Lydgate's *Troy Book*. The first four names are of those who came to the aid of Menelaus when Helen was first abducted (*TB* II.4435-4441); the next eleven are drawn from the Greek character descriptions, or "Portraits" (*TB* II.4509-5054), while the rest come from the actual Catalogue of Ships (*TB* II.5105-5198) with a few names from the Catalogue of Trojan Allies (*TB* II.7621-7817) erroneously tacked onto the end.

This amalgamation leads to the sons of Aesculapius, Machaon and Podalirius, appearing twice—as "Makary" and "Pollydamus" in the "Portraits" section, and later as "Mathaon and Pollidrus" in the "Catalogue of Ships" section. Oilean and Telamonian Ajax also become three characters: "King Cylyus, King Arax and King Telamus". The "King Tendalus" who sits between Diomedes and Agamemnon presents something of a puzzle; Combellack suggests he is the Rhodian Tlepolemus, or more likely a duplicated Patroclus, who is given as "Tantalus" in the Greek Portraits. His proximity to Diomedes also raises the possibility that he represents the Argive King Sthenelus

* C. R B. Combellack, "The Composite Catalogue of *The Sege of Troye*", *Speculum* vol. 26, no. 4 (1951): pp. 624-634

("Thelemus" in *Troy Book*), who was never far from the side of his fellow veteran of the Second Theban War.

Due to its four separate points of origin, the catalogue of the *Rawlinson Prose Siege of Troy* requires two extra tables to properly explain, listing the Greek character portraits and the Catalogue of Trojan Allies, respectively.

Homer's *Iliad*	Dares Phrygius
Agamemnon of Mycenae: 100	Agamemnon of Mycenae: 100
Menelaus of Lacedaemon: 60	Menelaus of Sparta: 60
Arcesilaus, Prothoenor, Peneleos, Leïtus & Clonius of Boeotia: 50	Arcesilaus & Prothoenor of Boeotia: 50
Ascalaphus & Ialmenus of the Minyans: 30	Ascalaphus & Ialmenus of Orchomenus: 30
Epistrophus & Schedius of Phocis: 40	Epistrophus & Schedius of Phocis: 40
Telamonian Ajax (& Teucer) of Salamis: 12	Telamonian Ajax & Teucer of Salamis; Amphimachus, Diores, Thalpius & Polyxenus of Buprasion: 40
Amphimachus, Diores, Thalpius & Polyxenus of Buprasion and Elis: 40	Antiphus & Amphimachus of Elis: 11
Nestor of Pylos: 90	Nestor of Pylos: 80
Thoas of Aetolia: 40	Thoas of Aetolia: 40
Nireus of Syme: 3	Nireus of Syme: 53
Oilean Ajax of Locris: 40	Oilean Ajax of Locris: 37
Antiphus & Phidippus of Nisryus, Calydna, et al.: 30	Antiphus & Phidippus of Calydna: 30
Idomeneus & Meriones of Crete: 80	Idomeneus & Meriones of Crete: 80
Odysseus of the Cephallenians: 12	Ulysses of Ithaca: 12
Eumelus of Pherae: 11	Eumelus of Pherae: 10
Podarces (prev. Protesilaus) of Phylace: 40	Protesilaus & Podarces of Phylace: 40
Podalirius & Machaon of Tricca, et al.: 30	Podalirius & Machaon of Tricca: 32
Achilles of Phthia, Hellas, et al.: 50	Achilles & Patroclus of Phthia: 50
Tlepolemus of Rhodes: 9	Tlepolemus of Rhodes: 9
Eurypylus of Ormenion, et al.: 40	Eurypylus of Ormenion: 40
Polypoetes & Leonteus of Argissa, et al.: 40	Polypoetes & Leonteus of Argissa: 40
Diomedes, Euryalus & Sthenelus of Argos: 80	Diomedes, Euryalus & Sthenelus of Argos: 80
Medon (prev. Philoctetes) of Meliboea, et al: 7	Philoctetes of Meliboea: 7
Guneus of Cyphus & Dodona: 22	Guneus of Cyphus: 21
Prothous of Magnesia: 40	Prothous of Magnesia: 40
Agapenor of Arcadia: 60	Agapenor of Arcadia: 40
Menestheus of Athens: 50	Menestheus of Athens: 50
Elephenor of Euboea: 40	*(Palamedes of Cormos: 30)*[*]
Meges of Dulichium: 40	*(Creneus of Pylos: 22)*[†]
Total: 1,186	Total: 1,122[‡]

[*] Not included in the total, as he arrived after the initial muster at Athens.

[†] Appears in some medieval manuscripts.

[‡] The text states 1,130 ships (*Excidio Trojae Historia*, 14).

Seege of Troye, MS. Lincoln's Inn	*Seege of Troye*, MS. Harley
Sir Agaman of Mestene: 50	Sir Agamanoun of Messen: 60
Sir Menolay, King of Greece: 500(?)	Sir Monaly, King of Greece: 100
Sir Archelay of Boys: 50	Sir Archeley of Boys: 50
Sir Astolope of Erkmer: 30	Sir Askelop of Orkemere: 40
Sir Etrop of Paladyde: 40	—
Sir Aiax of Salamayn: 40	Sir Pollex & Sir Talamon of Antaton: 80
Sir Ancipe of Alyde: 15	—
Sir Nestour of Pyle: 80	Sir Hectour of Peyle: 80
Sir Tholas of Tholy: 33	—
—	—
Sir Castor of Locry: 40	—
Sir Ancipe of Caladoun: 30	—
Sir Edomeyne of Grete: 80	—
Sir Ulex 15	Sir Eluxes of Parpachy: 50
Sir Ampedy of Pery: 10	—
Sir Podam of Calapy: 34; Sir Prestolay: 40	Sir Portislay of Polleke: 40
Sir Polinestor: 20	—
—	The Lord Parpadode: 40
Sir Theofele of Rode	Sir Tolomew
Sir Ermupil: 15	—
Sir Polipete of Empy: 80	Sir Anys: 60
—	—
Sir Philete of Melebow: 7	—
Sir Ywain of Cipre: 20	Sir Sennes of Cypres: 21
Sir Prestolay of Manassy: 40	—
Sir Sarpenor of Barbary: 40	—
Sir Monstow of Arbady: 50	—
Sir Namply of Palamyde: 30	—
Sir Dares of Parchy: 50	—
Total: 1,439(?)*	Total: 740†

* LI says 1,255, but does not state how many Menelaus actually brought to Troy—only that he constructed 500, some of which may have been distributed among other lords.

† The MS. Harl. 525 says 1,225 ships.

Benoît's *Roman de Troie*	**Guido's *Historia***
Agamennon de Miceines: 100	Agamenon de Mecenarum: 100
Menelaus de Parte: 60	Menelaus de Spartem: 60
Archelaus & Prothenor de Boëce: 50	Archelaus et Prothenor de Boecie: 50
Ascalaphus & Almenus d'Orcomenie: 30	Ascalafus et Helimus de Cythomenie: 30
Epistrophus & Scedius de Phocidis: 50	Epistrophus et Tedius de Forcidis: 50
Telamonius Aïaus, Teücer, Amphimac, Dorion, Polixenart & Theseüs de Salemine 50	Thelamonius Ayax, Teucer, Amphiacus, Dorion et Theseus de Salemina: 50
Antipus & Amphimaus d'Elide: 11	Anthipus et Amphimacus de Hesida: 11
Nestor de Pyle: 80	Nestor de Pilon: 50
Thoas de Tolias: 50	Thoas de Tholie: 50
Hunerius d'Essimiëis: 43	Rex autem Deximais: 50
Oïleïus Aïaus de Logres: 37	Ayax Oyleus: 36
Antipus & Philitoas de Caledoine: 30	Amphymacus et Polibetes de Calcidoine: 30
Idomeneus & Merion de Crete: 80	Ydumeneus et Merion de Creta: 80
Ulixès d'Achaie: 50	Vlixes de Tracie: 50
Emelius de Pigris: 10	Melius de Pigris: 10
Proteselaus & Potarcus de Phylace: 50	Prothesilaus et Prothotacus de Phylarca: 50
Polidri & Machaon de Tricios: 32	Polidus et Machaon de Tricionico: 22
Achillès (& Patroclus) de Phice: 50	Achilles (et Patroclus) de Phites: 50
Telepolus de Rode: 10	Thelephalus de Rodon: 12
Euripilus d'Orcomenie: 50	Euripilus de Ortomenie: 50
Polibetes & Leontins de Larise: 60	Polipetes et Losius de Richa: 60
Diomedès, Eürialus & Sthelenus d'Arges: 80	Dyomedes, Eurialus et Thelenus de Argis: 80
Philotetès de Melibee: 7	Poliphebus: 7
Cuneus de Cipe: 11	Fineus: 11
Prothoïlus de Manese: 50	Prothoylus de Demenesa: 50
Agapenor de Capadie: 50	Capenor de Capadie: 50
Menesteüs d'Athenes: 50	—
(Palamedes: 30)	*(Palamides: 30)*
Crenos de Pise: 22	Treorius de Beisa: 22
Total: 1,253*	Total: 1,171†

* Benoît agrees with Dares Phrygius' 1,130 ships (ll.5601-5697).

† Guido says 1,222 ships (IX.56-7).

Lydgate's *Troy Book*	The *Rawlinson Prose Siege*
Agamenoun: 100	(Agamenon)*
Menelaus of Sparten: 60	(Menelay)
Archelaus & Prothenor of Boece: 50	—
Achalapus & Helymux of Sycomenye: 30	—
Epistrophus & Cedyus: 50	—
Thelamoun Aiax, Teuter, Amphiacus, Darion & Theseus of Solemyne: 50	(Arax & Telamus)†
Antipus & Amphymacus of Hesida: 11	Antiphis of Esida
Nestor of Pilon: 50	—
Thoas of Tholie	—
& the King of Daymes: 100‡	The King of Daymes
Thelamoun Cilleus: 36	(Cylyus)†
Amphimacus & Polibete of Calcedoyne: 30	Amphimachus & Pollibete
Ydumeus & Meryoun of Crete: 80	—
Vlixes of Trace: 50	(Vlixes)†
Mellyus: 10	—
Prothisalus & Perotacus of Philiarcha: 50	(Prothesilaus)†
Polidris & Methaon of Trycianyco: 22	Pollidrus & Mathaon
Achilles (& Patroclus) of Phices: 50	(Achilles & Patroclus)*
Thelapolus of Rodon: 20	—
—	—
Polibethes & Losius of Richa: 50	—
Diomede, Euryale & Thelemus of Arge: 80	(Dyomede),* Eriale
Polyphebus: 7	Polliphebus
Phyneus: 11	—
Prothoylus of Demenesa: 50	—
Carpenor of Capadie: 50	Capenor of Capady
—	—
(Palamydes: 30)	(Pallamydes)†
Trearyus of Beysa: 22	Trerarius of Beysa
Total: 1,119	

* These characters are not drawn from the Catalogue of Ships, but are those who (according to Lydgate, Guido, etc) first came to Menelaus when Helen was abducted.

† Taken from the Character Portraits—not the Catalogue of Ships.

‡ Lydgate combines the contingents of Thoas and Nireus (II.5135-5138).

Portraits in Lydgate/Dares	The *Rawlinson Prose Siege*
Eleyne (Helen)	—
Agamenoun (Agamemnon)	—
Menelay (Menelaus)	—
Achilles	—
Tantalus (Patroclus)	Tendalus(?)
Oyleus Aiax (Oilean Ajax)	Cylyus, Arax
Aiax Thelamonius (Telamonian Ajax)	Telamus
Vlixes (Ulysses)	Vlixes
Diomede	—
Nestor	—
Protheselaus (Protesilaus)	Prothesilaus
Neptolonius (Neoptolemus)	Neptolomys
Pallamydes (Palamedes)	Pallamydes
Polydamus (Podalirius)	Pollydamus
Machaon	Makary
Cryseyde (Cressida)	—
The King of Perce (Persia)*	The King of Parce
Priamus	—
Ector (Hector)	—
Dephebus (Deiphobus)	—
Elenus (Helenus)	—
Troylus (Troilus)	—
Paris	—
Eneas (Aeneas)	—
Anthenor (Antenor)	—
Pollydamas (Polydamas)	—
Meryon (Meriones)	—
Eccuba (Hecuba)	—
Andronomecha (Andromache)	—
Cassandra	—
Pollicene (Polyxena)	—

* Not in Dares—comes from Benoît's *Roman de Troie* (l.5271).

Trojan Allies in Lydgate/Dares	The *Rawlinson Prose Siege*
Pollydamas (Polydamas)	—
The King of Perse (Persia)	(The King of Parce)*
Pandarus, Thabor & Andrastus (Pandarus, Amphius & Adrastus of Zelia)	The King of Barbary
Carias of Coloson (Mopsus of Colophon)	Cariac of Coloson
Ymasus (Asius of Phrygia)	—
Amphimacus & Nestor (Amphimachus & Nastes of Caria)	—
Sparedoun & Glaucoun of Lycye (Sarpedon & Glaucus of Lycia)	—
Hupon & Epedus (Hippothous & Cupesus of Larissa)	—
Caphemus of Lycaoun; Remus of Tabaria (Euphemus of Ciconia)†	—
Pilex & Alcamus of Trace (Pirus & Acamas of Thrace)	Philex of Trace
Pretemissus & Stupex of Panonye (Pyraechmes & Astreopaeus of Paeonia)	—
Samus & Forcynus of Botyne (Ascanius & Phorcys of Phrygia)	Forcunus of Bosy
Anphimus & Miseres (Antiphus & Mesthles of Maeonia)	—
Philymene of Pafogonye on the river Tygre (Pylaemenes of Paphlagonia)	Philanyme of Tigre
Porses, Meryon & Sygamon‡ of Ethiope (Perses & Memnon of Ethiopia)	Porces & Sygamon of Ethiope
Theseus & Archilagus of Teremo (Rhesus & Archilochus of Thrace)	Terenes of Dares & Archiligus
Two kings of Agresta (Adrastus & Amphius of Adrestia)	Ampheus
Episterus & Boetes of Bitunye; Epistrophus of Lissynya (Epistrophus & Odius of Alizonia)§	Epistrophus

* Taken from the Character Portraits—not the list of Trojan Allies.

† Benoît's *Roman de Troie* splits Euphemus into two characters (ll.6695-6 & l.6713).

‡ Not in Dares.

§ Like Euphemus, Benoît makes two characters of Epistrophus (ll.6793-5 & ll.6893-5).

BIBLIOGRAPHY

Aeschylus, *The Oresteia: Agamemnon; The Libation Bearers; The Eumenides,* translated by Robert Fagles (New York: Penguin Books, 1984)

Apollodorus, *The Library,* translated by Sir James George Frazer (London: William Heinemann Ltd, 1921)

Apollonius of Rhodes, *Argonautica,* translated by E. V. Rieu (New York: Penguin Books, 1959)

Atwood, E. Bagby, "The Rawlinson Excidium Troie – A Study of Source Problems in Mediaeval Troy Literature", *Speculum* vol. 9, no. 4 (1934)

Atwood, E. Bagby, "The Story of Achilles in the Seege of Troye", *Studies in Philology* vol. 39, no. 3 (1942)

Atwood, E. Bagby and Virgil K. Whitaker (eds.), *Excidium Troiae* (Cambridge, MA: The Mediaeval Academy of America, 1944)

Barnicle, Mary Elizabeth, *The Seege or Battle of Troy: A Middle English Metrical Romance* (London: Oxford University Press, 1927)

Boccaccio, Giovanni, *Genealogie Deorum Gentilium Libri,* edited by Vincenzo Romano (Bari: *Gius. Laterza & Figli*, 1951)

Boccaccio, Giovanni, *Il Filostrato,* translated by Hubertis Cummings (Princeton, NJ: Princeton University Press, 1924)

Brie, Friedrich (ed.), "Zwei Mittelenglische Prosaromane: The Sege of Thebes und The Sege of Troy", *Herrig's Archiv,* vol. 130 (1913)

Burgess, Jonathan S., *The Tradition of the Trojan War in Homer and the Epic Cycle* (Baltimore, MD: Johns Hopkins University Press, 2003)

Cary, Earnest, *The Roman Antiquities of Dionysius of Halicarnassus* (Cambridge, MA: Harvard University Press, 1960)

Chaucer, Geoffrey, *Troilus and Criseyde,* edited by Barry Windeatt (Oxford: Oxford University Press, 1998)

Combellack, C. R. B., "The Composite Catalogue of *The Sege of Troye*", *Speculum* vol. 26, no. 4 (1951)

Davies, Malcolm, *The Greek Epic Cycle* (Bristol: Bristol Classical Press, 1989)

Delle Colonne, Guido, *Historia Destructionis Troiae,* edited by Nathaniel Edward Griffin (Cambridge, MA: Medieval Academy Books, 1936)

Delle Colonne, Guido, *Historia Destructionis Troiae,* translated by Mary Elizabeth Meek (Bloomington, IN: Indiana University Press, 1974)

De Sainte-Maure, Benoît, *Roman de Troie,* edited by Léopold Constans (Paris: Libraire De Firmin Didot Et Cie, 1904)

Diodorus Siculus, *Library of History: Books 2.35-4.58,* translated by C. H. Oldfather (Cambridge, MA: Harvard University Press, 1935)

Euripides, *Electra and Other Plays,* translated by John Davie (Penguin Books, 1999)

Euripides, *Medea and Other Plays,* translated by John Davie (Penguin Books, 2003)

Evelyn-White, H. G., (tran.), *Hesiod. Homeric Hymns. Epic Cycle. Homerica* (London: William Heinemann Ltd, 1914)

Frazer, R. M. (Jr.), (tran.), *The Trojan War. The Chronicles of Dictys of Crete and Dares the Phrygian* (Bloomington, IN: Indiana University Press, 1966)

Galli, Daniela, "Dionysius Scytobrachion's *Argonautica* and Valerius" in Antonios Augoustakis (ed.), *Flavian Poetry and its Greek Past* (Leiden: Brill, 2014)

Grant, Mary Amelia (tran.), *The Myths of Hyginus* (Lawrence, KS: University of Kansas Press, 1960)

Griffin, Nathaniel Edward, *Dares and Dictys, An Introduction to the Study of Medieval Versions of the Story of Troy* (Baltimore, MD: J. H. Furst Company, 1907)

Griffin, Nathaniel Edward, "The Greek Dictys", *The American Journal of Philology* vol. 29, no. 3 (1900)

Griffin, Nathaniel Edward, "The Sege of Troye", *PMLA* vol. 22, no. 1 (1907)

Homer, *The Iliad,* translated by A. T. Murray (London: William Heinemann Ltd, 1924)

Homer, *The Odyssey,* translated by A. T. Murray (London: William Heinemann Ltd, 1919)

Horace, *The Complete Odes and Epodes,* translated by David West (Oxford: Oxford University Press, 2008)

Kurath, Hans and Sherman Kuhn, *The Middle English Dictionary* (Ann Arbor, MI: University of Michigan Press, 1952)

Lefévre, Raoul and William Caxton, *The Recuyell of the Historyes of Troye,* edited by H. Oskar Sommer (London: David Nutt, 1894)

Lloyd-Jones, Hugh (tran.), *Sophocles: Fragments* (Cambridge, MA: Harvard University Press, 1996)

Louis-Jensen, Jonna (ed.), *Trójumanna Saga* (Copenhagen: Munksgaard, 1963)

Lydgate, John, *Lydgate's Troy Book,* edited by Henry Bergen (London: Kegan Paul, Trench, Trübner & Co., 1906)

Miklošic, Franc (ed.), *Trojanska Prica: Bugarski i Latinski* (Zagreb: Jugoslavenska Akademija Znanosti i Umjetnosti, 1870)

Ovid, *Metamorphoses,* translated by Brookes Moore (Boston, MA: Corn-hill Publishing Co., 1922)

Panton, Geo. A. and David Donaldson, *The Gest Hystoriale of the Destruction of Troy: An Alliterative Romance* (London: N. Trübner and Co., 1869)

Quintus Smyrnaeus, *Posthomerica,* translated by Alan James (Baltimore, MD: Johns Johns Hopkins University Press, 2004)

Smith, Leslie F., "The Thousand Ships", *L'antiquité Classique* vol. 49 (1980)

Statius, *Achilleid,* translated by J. H. Mozley (London: William Heinemann Ltd, 1928)

Thucydides, *The Peloponnesian War,* translated by Richard Crawley (London: J. M. Dent, 1910)

Torrey Harris, William and F. Sturges Allen (eds.), *Webster's New International Dictionary* (Springfield, MA: G. & C. Merriam Company, 1913)

Turville-Petre, Thorlac, "The Author of The Destruction of Troy", *Medium Ævum* vol. 57, no. 2 (1988)

Valerius Flaccus, *Argonautica,* translated by J. H. Mozley (Cambridge, MA: Harvard University Press, 1934)

Virgil, *The Aeneid,* translated by C. Day Lewis (Oxford: Oxford University Press, 1998)

Von Würzburg, Konrad, *Der Trojanische Kreig*, translated by Adelbert von Keller (Stuttgart: Stuttgart Literarische Verein, 1858)

Wager, C. H. A. (ed.), *The Seege of Troye: Edited From MS. Harl. 525* (New York: Macmillan, 1899)

Weber, Henry (ed.), *Metrical Romances of the Thirteenth, Fourteenth, and Fifteenth Centuries* (Edinburgh: George Ramsay and Co., 1810)

West, Martin L., *Greek Epic Fragments* (Cambridge, MA: Harvard University Press, 2003)

Wülfing, J. Ernst (ed.), *The Laud Troy Book: A Romance of About 1400 A.D.* (London: Kegan Paul, Trench, Trübner & Co., 1902)

Zietsch, A. (ed.), "Zwei Mittelenglische Bearbeitungen der Historia de Excidio Trojae des Phrygiers Dares", *Herrig's Archiv,* vol. 72 (1884)

INDEX

Achilles, *leader of the Myrmidons*, 47-62, 64-8, 70-9, 85, 88, 110, 113-7, 119
Aeëtes, *king of Colchis*, 96, 100
Aeneas, *Trojan hero of the Aeneid*, 82, 83, 85, 105, 117-9
Aeson, *father of Jason*, 93
Aetolia, *region of Greece*, 37
Africa, 14, 107
Agamemnon, *king of Mycenae*, 33-4, 38-40, 47, 69, 110-2, 116
Agapenor, *king of Arcadia*, 36, 110
Ajax, *son of Oileus*, 38, 110
Ajax, *son of Telamon*, 36, 80-2, 110
Alexander (Paris), *son of Priam*, 9, 13, 17, 24-31, 42-3, 46, 66, 68-9, 73, 77-81, 83
Alexander the Great, *Macedonian king*, 26
Antenor, *Trojan elder*, 13-5, 82-5, 105-6, 112-3, 117-9
Antenorean, *one of the gates of Troy*, 104
Anthedon(?), *kingdom of Telamon and Polyxenus in MS. Harl. 525*, 36
Antiphus, *Calydnian leader*, 110
Antiphus, *Elean leader*, 37, 110, 112
Antiphus, *Maeonian leader*, 110
Apollo, *god of archery, prophecy, et al.*, 22, 38-9
Arcadia, *region of Greece*, 36, 110
Arcesilaus, *Boeotian leader*, 35
Archilochus, *Thracian leader*, 110, 112
Aristotle, *Greek philosopher*, 27
Ascalaphus, *king of Orchomenus*, 35
Asia, 107

Barbary, *region of North Africa*, 110
Boeotia, *region of Greece*, 35, 110

Calchas, *father of Cressida*, 112, 113, 118
Calydna, *Anatolian city*, 37
Cassandra, *daughter of Priam*, 105
Castor, *twin brother of Pollux*, 4, 14, 26, 101-2, 106, 109
Colophon, *Greek city*, 110
Cressida, *daughter of Calchas*, 113
Crete, *Greek island*, 37
Creusa, *wife of Aeneas*, 105
Cyphus, *Greek city*, 35
Cythera, *Greek island*, 26

Dardanian, *one of the gates of Troy*, 104
Dares Phrygius, *author of the Excidio Trojae Historia*, 1, 33-4, 39, 93, 119
David, *king of Israel*, 26
Deidamia, *mother of Pyrrhus*, 50-1
Deiphobus, *son of Priam*, 104, 111
Colchis, *kingdom on the Black Sea*, 94-6
Diana, *goddess of the hunt*, 107
Diomedes, *king of Argos*, 110
Diores, *Elean leader*, 112

Elis, *Greek city*, 37, 110

Epistrophus, *Halizone leader*, 110
Epistrophus, *Phocian leader*, 36, 112
Ethiopia, *region of Africa*, 110
Eumelus, *Pheraean leader*, 37
Europe, 107
Euryalus, *companion of Diomedes*, 110
Eurypylus, *king of Thessaly*, 38

Ganymede, *Trojan prince*, 105
Greece, 1-5, 7-8, 14, 16-7, 24-7, 30-3, 37-8, 40, 43-4, 46-7, 50, 53-4, 57, 61, 63, 66-70, 72, 78-81, 83-5, 87-89, 95, 100-3, 105, 107, 109, 116, 119
Greek(s)/Grecian(s), 1, 3, 7, 13, 15, 25, 32, 38, 40, 46-7, 53, 69, 88, 102, 105-6, 109-113, 115-9
Guido delle Colonne, *author of the Historia Destructionis Troiae*, 93, 94, 96, 103, 119
Guneus, *leader of the Aenianes and Perrhaebians*, 35

Hector, *son of Priam*, 9, 13, 16-8, 20, 24, 42-6, 48, 54-64, 67, 70, 73, 77, 81, 87, 104, 106-7, 109-115, 117
Hecuba, *queen of Troy*, 9, 13, 73, 104, 114-5, 117, 119
Helen, *queen of Sparta*, 26, 28, 30-2, 40, 66-7, 81, 88-9, 101, 106, 108, 109, 118-9
Helenus, *son of Priam*, 104
Hercules, *Greek hero*, 3-8, 14, 15, 26, 71, 95, 99, 100, 101, 102
Hesione, *daughter of Laomedon*, 7, 9, 14, 26, 102-3, 105-6, 118

Idomeneus, *king of Crete*, 37
Ilian, *one of the gates of Troy*, 104

Jaconites, *fictional city of Colchis*, 96
Jason, *leader of the Argonauts*, 1-4, 6, 7, 93-100, 102
Jesus, *Christian prophet*, 13, 42, 81
Jupiter, *god of thunder*, 13, 19, 21-2
Juno, *queen of the Olympian gods*, 21-23

King of Troy, 1-4, 6, 8-9, 27-8, 31, 40, 42, 44, 57, 63, 68, 73, 78, 95, 105

Laomedon, *king of Troy*, 3-5, 7, 71, 95, 100-3, 105
Locris, *region of Greece*, 38
Lycomedes, *king of Scyros*, 50

Machaon, *son of Aesculapius*, 110, 116
Magnesia, *region of Greece*, 36
Medea, *princess of Colchis*, 93, 96-8, 100
Meliboea, *Greek city*, 37
Menelaus, *king of Sparta*, 26-7, 29, 32, 38-9, 46, 54, 67, 70, 78, 82, 84, 85, 89, 107-110
Menestheus, *king of Athens*, 36, 45
Mercury, *herald of the gods*, 19, 20
Messene, *Greek city*, 101
Minerva, *goddess of wisdom*, 118
Mohammed, *Islamic prophet*, 22, 23, 54, 55
Mopsus, *Colophonian leader*, 110
Mycenae, *Greek city*, 34
Myrmidons, *the followers of Achilles*, 85

Nectanebo, *Egyptian pharaoh*, 27
Neoptolemus (Pyrrhus), *son of Achilles*, 85, 88, 110
Nestor, *king of Pylos*, 4, 14, 26, 35, 101

Oileus, *father of Ajax*, 110
Olympias, *mother of Alexander the Great*, 27
Orchomenus, *Greek city*, 35
Ottoman Sea (Aegean Sea?), 25

Phocis, *region of Greece*, 36
Palamedes, *Euboean leader*, 38, 47, 48, 110, 114
Pallas (Minerva), *goddess of wisdom*, 21-3
Parchy (Sparta?), *Greek city*, 35, 49, 50
Paris, *son of Priam*, 9, 11, 13, 17, 19, 22-5, 27-32, 42-3, 46, 55, 66, 68, 69, 74, 79-83, 87, 104, 106-9, 111, 113-7
Patroclus, *companion of Achilles*, 35, 44-5, 110, 112
Peleus, *king of Phthia*, 48
Pelias, *king of Iolcus*, 2, 93-4, 100-2, 105
Peloponnese, *region of Greece*, 2
Perses, *Ethiopian leader*, 110
Persia, 110
Pherae, *Greek city*, 37
Phidippus, *Calydnian leader*, 110, 116
Philoctetes, *Meliboean leader*, 37, 94, 110
Phorcys, *Phrygian leader*, 110
Phrygia, *region of Anatolia*, 9, 95
Pirus, *Thracian leader*, 110, 114
Podalirius, *son of Aesculapius*, 36, 110
Podarces, *brother of Protesilaus*, 35
Pollux, *twin brother of Castor*, 4, 14, 26, 101, 106, 109
Polydorus, *son of Priam*, 105
Polypoetes, *Lapith leader*, 35, 61
Polyxena, *daughter of Priam*, 64-5, 74, 75, 87, 105, 114-6, 119
Polyxenus, *Elean leader*, 36
Priam(us), *king of Troy*, 9, 13, 15, 17, 24, 28, 40-2, 54-5, 58, 61, 63-6, 73, 75, 79, 82, 84, 87, 103-7, 109-115, 117-9
Protesilaus, *king of Phylace*, 38, 44, 110-1
Prothous, *Magnesian leader*, 36
Pylaemenes, *king of Paphlagonia*, 110
Pyle/Pylos, *Greek island*, 35, 101
Pyrrhus (Neoptolemus), *son of Achilles*, 85-8

Rhesus, *king of Thrace*, 110
Rhodes, *Greek island*, 37

Salamis, *Greek island*, 36
Saturnus, *an "elven lady"*, 19, 20
Scaean, *one of the gates of Troy*, 104
Sigamon, *brother of Memnon*, 110
Simoent, *fictional Trojan port*, 101, 110
Solomon, *king of Israel*, 26
Sparta, *Greek city*, 35, 49, 101
Syme, *Greek island*, 110

Telamon, *father of Ajax*, 4, 14, 26, 36, 101-2, 105-6, 110
Tenedos, *Anatolian island*, 101, 108-9
Thessaly, *region of Greece*, 35, 93, 107
Thetis, *mother of Achilles*, 49
Thoas, *Aetolian leader*, 37
Thrace, *region between Greece and Anatolia*, 110
Thymbraean, *one of the gates of Troy*, 104
Tigris, *Mesapotamian river*, 110
Tlepolemus, *king of Rhodes*, 37
Treorius, *king of Beysa*, 110
Troilus, *son of Priam*, 9, 66, 68-9, 72, 73, 77, 104, 109, 111, 113-6
Trojan, *one of the gates of Troy*, 104
Trojan(s), 2, 4, 9, 13, 15, 29, 69, 86, 102, 104, 109-119
Troy, 1, 3-5, 7, 9-12, 16, 24-6, 30, 36-42, 44, 47, 53-5, 57, 61-3, 65, 71, 73, 79, 81-2, 84, 87, 89, 90, 95, 100-3, 105-6, 108-113, 118-9
Tyndaris, *Sicilian city*, 101

Ulysses, *hero of the Odyssey*, 37, 110

Venus, *goddess of love*, 19, 21-4

INDEX

D. M. Smith is a serial procrastinator and occasional writer and editor. He was born in Hamilton, New Zealand in 1983, and studied Theatre at the University of Waikato. His interests include Greek mythology, all things vintage and antique, English literature, the music of Jethro Tull, tea, and toilet humour. His first novel, *Munley Priory: A Gothic Story* was published in 2016.

He lives in Horotiu, New Zealand, and is married with five cats.

Follow **@d.m.smith.authorpage** on Facebook to interact with the author and receive information on upcoming titles.

Made in the USA
Middletown, DE
23 February 2023

25429849R00104